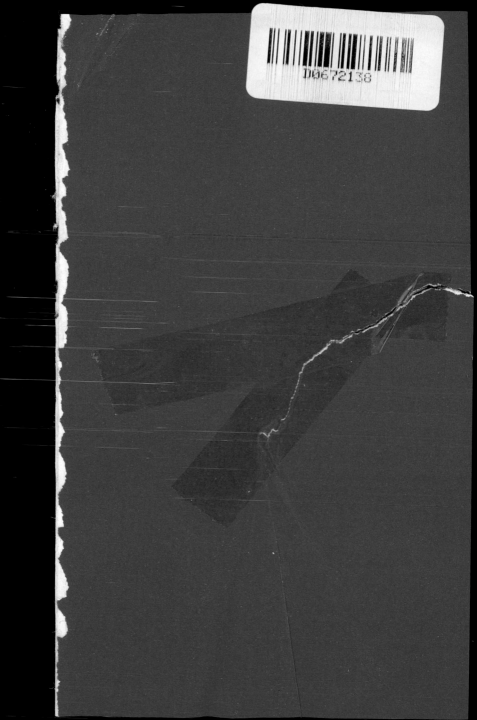

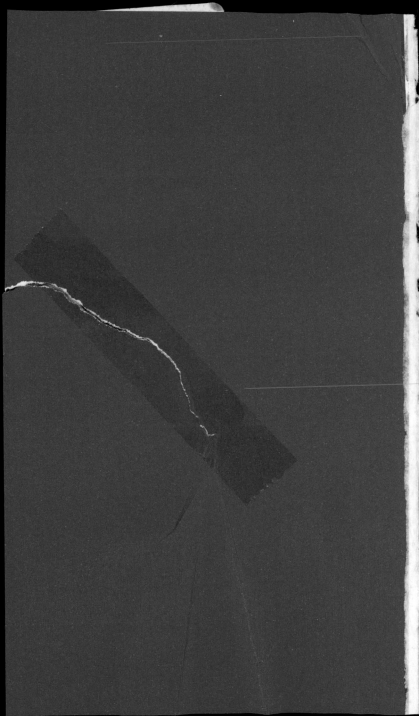

Hg2 Prague

A Hedonist's guide to
Prague

Written and photographed by
Paul Sullivan

A Hedonist's guide to Prague

Managing director – Tremayne Carew Pole
Marketing director – Sara Townsend
Series editor – Catherine Blake
Design – Katy Platt
Maps – Richard Hale
Repro – Dorchester Typesetting
Printers – Printed in China by Leo
Publisher – Filmer Ltd

Additional writing – Wendy Wrangham, Tremayne Carew Pole
Additional photography – Tremayne Carew Pole, Andrea Plechacova,
Maie Crumpton

Email – info@hg2.com
Website – www.hg2.com

2nd Edition
First published in the United Kingdom in October 2007 by
Filmer Ltd
47 Filmer Road,
London SW6 7JJ

ISBN – 1-905428-09-X / 978-1-905428-09-0

Hg2 Prague

CONTENTS

How to...

A *Hedonist's guide to Prague* is broken down into easy to use sections: Sleep, Eat, Drink, Snack, Party, Culture, Shop, Play and Info. In each of these sections you will find detailed reviews and photographs. At the front of the book you will find an introduction to the city and an overview map, followed by introductions to the four main areas and more detailed maps. On each of these maps you will see the places that we have reviewed, laid out by section, highlighted on the map with a symbol and a number. To find out about a particular place simply turn to the relevant section, where all entries are listed alphabetically. Alternatively, browse through a specific section (e.g. Eat) until you find a restaurant that you like the look of. Next to your choice will be a small coloured dot – each colour refers to a particular area of the city. Simply turn to the relevant map to discover the location.

Updates

Hg2 have developed a network of journalists in each city to review the best hotels, restaurants, bars, clubs, etc., and to keep track of the latest developments – new places open up all the time, while others simply fade away or just go out of style. To access our free updates as well as the content of each guide, simply log onto our website www.Hg2.com and register. We welcome your help. If you have any comments or recommendations, please feel free to email us at info@hg2.com.

Book your hotel on Hg2.com

We believe that the key to a great city break is choosing the right hotel. Our unique site now enables you to browse through our selection of hotels, using the interactive maps to give you a good feel for the area as well as the nearby restaurants, bars, sights, etc. before you book. Hg2 has formed partnerships with the hotels featured in our guide to bring them to readers at the lowest possible price. Our site now incorporates special offers from selected hotels, as well as a diary of interesting events taking place, 'Inspire Me'.

The concept

A Hedonist's guide to Prague is designed to appeal to a more urbane and stylish traveller. The kind of traveller who is interested in gourmet food, elegant hotels and seriously chic bars – the traveller who feels the need to explore, shop and pamper themselves away from the crowds.

Our aim is to give you an insider's knowledge of a city, to make you feel like a well-heeled, sophisticated local and to take you to the most fashionable places in town to rub shoulders with the local glitterati.

In today's world work rules our life, and weekends away are few and far between; when we do manage to get away we want to have as much fun and to relax as much as possible with the minimum amount of stress. This guide is all about maximizing time. There is a photograph of each place we feature, so before you go you know exactly what you are getting into; choose a restaurant or bar that suits you and your needs.

We pride ourselves on our independence and our integrity. We eat in all the restaurants, drink in all the bars and go wild in the nightclubs – all totally incognito. We charge no one for the privilege of appearing in the guide, and every place is reviewed and included at our discretion.

We feel cities are best enjoyed by soaking up the atmosphere: wander the streets, indulge in some retail therapy, re-energize yourself with a massage and then get ready to eat like a king and party hard on the local scene.

Prague

One of the most majestic and mysterious cities in Europe, Prague acts as a magnet for tourists who come from all over the world to witness the peerless beauty of this 'city of a hundred spires'. The city is the culmination of many hundred years of architecture, and its main allure lies in its narrow, medieval streets, baroque, neo-Renaissance, Art Nouveau and Art Deco edifices, and its cutting-edge, contemporary design.

One of the joys of Prague is its size. Unlike unwieldy, unknowable cities such as London or Paris, one can grasp the dimensions of Prague fairly firmly – even though it can be impenetrable in other ways – and getting to know the many sights and stories of its historical centre is an exquisitely intimate pleasure.

However, the centre itself is fashioned from several districts. The heart of the city encompasses Hradčany, Malá Strana, Staré Město, Nové Město and Josefov and, as in so many other European cities, those who inhabit these areas tend to be affluent locals and ex-pats. Everyone else lives in the surrounding cadastral districts of Vinohrady, Žižkov and Smíchov, where the architecture is less remarkable and English less widely spoken – and the inhabitants are said to possess oodles of character.

The city's colourful, turbulent and majestic history – which features everything from magic-loving monarchs and dastardly defen-

estrations to velvet revolutions and White Mountain battles – combined with its easily accessible centre and awe-inspiring beauty, has made it popular with the romantically and culturally minded.

Cheap flights, cheap booze and the proliferation of adult clubs has also made it a fashionable destination for marauding stag parties. Hence your arm-in-arm stroll through Old Town Square may be interrupted by the occasional group of beer-swilling males in garish (but matching) T-shirts. Discerning visitors should not be alarmed. This guide's aim is to steer you into the empyrean embrace of Prague's more bespoke realms, and away from the kind of mass tourism that has blighted the city's reputation these last few years.

There are plenty of upmarket options, too: Prague has come an incredibly long way since the fall of Communism. Where there were once a few grand hotels and a smattering of mediocre eateries, today's Prague offers gourmet food in classy surroundings and sophisticated cafés, trendy cocktail bars and cutting-edge nightclubs.

To enjoy the city at its finest, however, spend some time wandering the cobbled lanes and exploring the nooks and crannies. The city's diversions may lie in its new breed of designer venues, but its history can be found in the streets and houses, the churches and statues as much as within the more famous Gothic churches and grand museums.

Prague city map

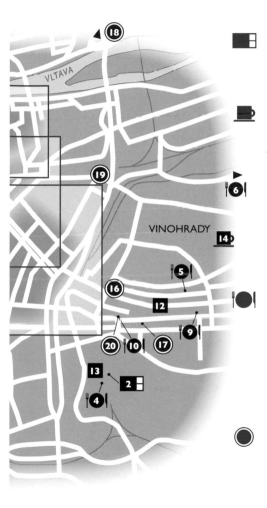

DRINK

12. Techtle Mechtle
13. Zvonařka

SLEEP

1. Andels
2. Le Palais
3. Riverside

SNACK

14. Sahara Café

VLTAVA

VINOHRADY

EAT

4. L'Ardoise
5. Aromi
6. Atelier
7. Le Bistrot de Marlene
8. Brasserie Ullmann
9. Mozaika
10. Sahara Café
11. Soho

PARTY

15. Akropolis
16. Big Sister
17. Le Clan
18. K5
19. Mecca
20. Studio 54

Staré Město

the Old Town

The Old Town is the centre of historic Prague. Tourists flock to Old Town Square to admire the architecture and gaze at the Astronomical Clock's hourly morality play. The narrow, cobbled streets epitomize the timelessness of the city, and lure you into an exploration of its enigmatic courtyards and alleyways.

Inevitably, the district's charismatic appeal means that it is also awash with sightseers. The Royal Way, which runs from Námestí Republiky to Charles Bridge, is often crowded with tour groups following women with umbrellas yelling out instructions and piecemeal histories.

If you want to discover the real essence of the Old Town, it's best to detach yourself from the obvious routes and attempt spontaneous detours and back routes; you really can't get too lost, so don't worry about taking wrong turns.

While the Old Town boasts many exceptional hotels, bars, cafés and restaurants, it is generally more geared towards themed and 'authentic'

tourism than the rest of the city. Owing to the narrowness of the streets and the diminutive size of the buildings, hotels here tend to be cosy and intimate rather than imposing and grand.

One of the best in the city is the Hotel U Prince, directly on Old Town Square, whose comfortable, ornate rooms and traditional elegance reflect Prague's past grandeur. Nearby Residence Retězová is a collection of apartments in an old townhouse, offering the visitor both comfort and independence.

Many of the restaurants within the Old Town lure tourists in with the 'authentic' card, but they're often disappointing. Flambée, a formal, designer cellar restaurant serving Czech–French fusion food, is a distinct (and distinguished) exception; Parnas, a glorious old world, Art Deco spot with stunning views over the river and Castle, is also recommended; and V Zátiší, a Czech–French hybrid set on the perfectly charming Betlemska square, has been rated by critics as one of the best in the country.

There are noteworthy cafés in Old Town, but while it can be pleasant to lunch here and bask in the sunshine with the crowds, you might be better off elsewhere. Café Café enjoys views of the Estates Theatre, offers a great cup of coffee and plays host to the Czech glitterati. Nostress is a stylish spot, tucked away just behind Old Town Square; and Café Montmartre epitomizes the nostalgic Bohemian chic of yesteryear.

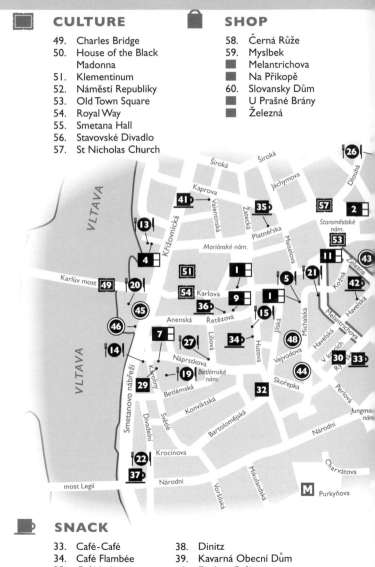

Staré Město (the Old Town) local map

PARTY

43. AghaRTA Jazz Centrum
44. La Fabrique
45. Karlovy Lázně
46. Klub Lavka
47. Ungelt Jazz & Blues Club
48. U Stare Pani

0   125   250m

Ⓜ Metro Station

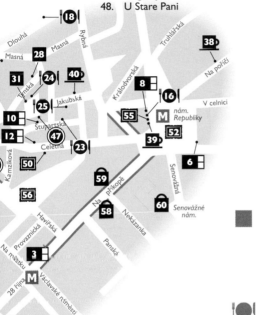

DRINK

28. Bar and Books
29. Duende
30. K.U. Café
31. Legends
32. Monarch Wine Bar

EAT

13. Allegro
14. Bellevue
15. Flambée
16. Francouszka
17. Khajuraho
18. Lary Fary
19. Lehka Hlava
20. Mlynec
21. U Modré Kachničky
22. Parnas
23. La Provence
24. Rbyí Trh
25. Le Saint Jacques
26. Yami
27. V Zátiší

SLEEP

1. U Červené Boty
2. Černý Slon
3. Floor Hotel
4. Four Seasons
5. Iron Gate
6. K+K Hotel Centrale
7. Pachtuv Palace
8. Paříz
9. Residence Řetežova
10. Ungelt
11. U Prince
12. Ventana Hotel Prague

Nové Město
the New Town

Prague's New Town is not what you might expect. Instead of the concrete, glass and neon signs the name might suggest, you get stunning baroque and Art Nouveau architecture. Founded in 1348 by Charles IV, the New Town has continued to grow and develop, and is now in part typified by the 1920s and 1930s showpiece architecture of Wenceslas Square.

Nové Město is essentially an extension of the Old Town, but its streets are wider, and its focus falls less on the tourist trade and more on day-to-day Czech life. However, since it's still a chic and expensive area, its inhabitants are usually wealthy – everybody else lives further out, in Žižkov, Vinohrady and beyond.

Within the New Town are two distinct areas, separated by Wenceslas Square. To the west is the trendy district known as SoNa ('South of the National Theatre'). Here you'll find Prague's designers, writers and media types, drawn to the area by the more alternative scene vibrant in the area's many bars and restaurants.

These establishments fall into two categories: simple, shabby–chic places with old-fashioned décor, smoky air and heavy cooking;

and the new breed of designer cafés serving frothy coffees, Asian fusion food and Californian wines.

Wenceslas Square is a dichotomy of styles: beautiful Art Nouveau edifices fight with faceless Soviet-era department stores. This is Prague's Leicester Square, packed with tourists, large international shops and several strip joints. Commerce is the name of the game, from the mainstream retailers to the hookers and dealers who hang around the bottom end of the square.

At the top end are the National Museum and the State Opera. And to the east is a quieter, more residential area where small shops cater for local clientele. There are also some stunning buildings, glamorous hotels and the much-vaunted Mucha Museum. Na Příkopě, the shopping street that forms the border between New and Old Town, offers four or five shopping centres as well as some familiar high-street stores.

Notable restaurants in this part of town include Zahrada v Opeře, a chic and stylish establishment that is part of the State Opera complex, and Kogo, the haunt of politicians, tourists and well-placed ex-pats.

The New Town is also the home of the luxurious Carlo IV, arguably the Czech Republic's most opulent hotel, which contrasts dramatically with the humdrum huddle of hotels dotted around the main square, which are mostly soulless sorts that cater to tour groups and business conferences.

⊙ PARTY

25. Ambassador Casino
26. Atlas
27. Casino Palace Savarin
28. Darling Cabaret
29. Duplex
30. Goldfingers
31. Lucerna Music Bar
32. Radost FX
33. Reduta
34. Solidni Nejistota

🛍 SHOP

41. Koruna Palace
42. Lucerna Passage
◼ Jungmannova Náměstí
◼ Wenceslas Square

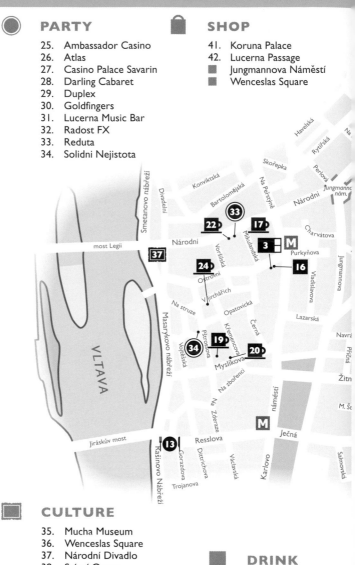

▦ CULTURE

35. Mucha Museum
36. Wenceslas Square
37. Národní Divadlo
38. Státní Opera
39. Praha 1 & 2
40. Slovansky Dům

◼ DRINK

15. Inn Ox Bar
16. Ultramarin

Nové Město (the New Town) local map

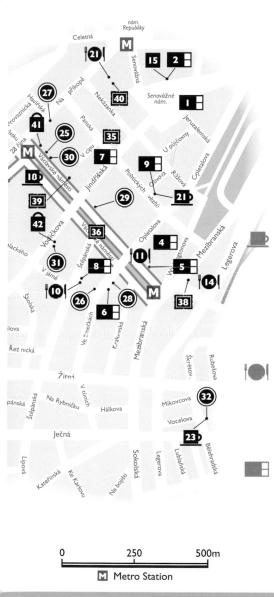

SNACK

17. Café Louvre
18. Dobrá Čajovna
19. Globe
20. Lemon Leaf
21. Noodles
22. le Patio
23. Radost FX
24. Universal

EAT

10. Alcron
11. Hot
12. Kogo
13. La Perle de Prague
14. Zahrada v Opeře

SLEEP

1. 987 Prague
2. Carlo IV
3. Elite
4. Esplanade
5. Jalta
6. K+K Hotel Fenix
7. Palace
8. Radisson SAS
9. Yasmin

0   250   500m

M Metro Station

Hradčany & Malá Strana

the Castle District & Lesser Quarter

Hradčany and Malá Strana are two small districts that rise up above the river to the west of Charles Bridge. Much like the rest of Prague, they are steeped in history and draw a large concentration of sightseers determined to explore the hilly, cobbled streets and feast their eyes on the fabulous architecture.

Prague's most recognizable landmark is its castle; perched above the city like a watchful eagle, it has been the centre of government for centuries. Over this period, the castle's complex has expanded into a mini-city. Within its walls, churches, galleries and museums attract visitors from around the world, while heads of state come to meet the government and president.

The Castle and its immediate environs make up the Hradčany district, which also includes the Strahov Monastery and the Loreto Chapel. Aside from the area's cultural allure, it doesn't have too much else to offer. However, the Savoy Hotel and Domus Henrici are perched above the Castle, while the more bucolic U Raka lurks beneath; all provide a good base from which to explore this region.

Malá Strana, like the Old Town, is not quite so busy with tourists. Forming the western approach to Charles Bridge, the 'Lesser Quarter' acts as a funnel for visitors

crossing the bridge and continuing on up the Royal Way towards the Castle. Consequently the busy Nerudova and Mostecká thoroughfares can be bottlenecked by groups gathering around shops to ogle model houses, gawp at frightening marionettes and contemplate Prague Drinking Team T-shirts.

It's worth taking the time to wander off the beaten track and go exploring. Losing yourself in the small side streets is a good way to encounter interesting atmospheres and discover parts of the city's history as well as its cafés and restaurants. The terrace restaurant of U Zlaté Studně hotel, for example, offers fabulous views and gourmet cuisine in serene and little visited surroundings, and the wonderful Mandarin Hotel, with its stunning spa, is also in the area. Café enthusiasts might want to seek out the delightful Cukr Káva Limonáda.

Malá Strana has a plentiful selection of hotels to choose from. The most intriguing include the Aria, a masterpiece of musical innovation, and the Alchymist, which adopts a more magical theme. Likewise there are many restaurants where you can indulge your culinary fantasies. A number of places have recently opened to lure in sightseers tempted by the idea of 'authentic' traditional cooking, but there's little point in bothering with these when restaurants such as Kampa Park and Hergetova Cihelná can offer you excellent food in beautiful locations.

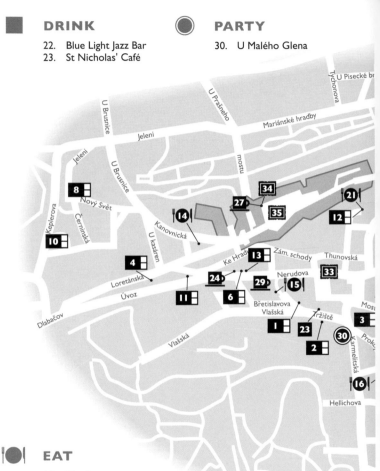

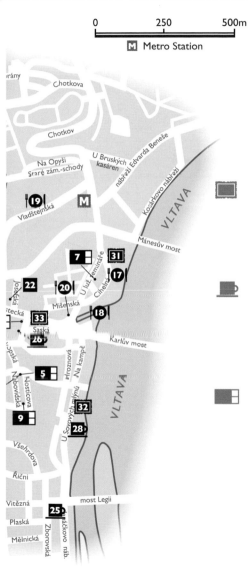

0   250   500m

M Metro Station

CULTURE

31. Franz Kafka Museum
32. Kampa Museum
33. Royal Way
34. Prague Castle
35. Prague Castle (concert)

SNACK

24. Café Carolina
25. Café Savoy
26. Cukr Káva Limonáda
27. Lobkowwicz
28. Sovový Mlýny
29. U Zeleného Čaje

SLEEP

1. Alchymist Grand
2. Aria Hotel
3. Domus Balthasar
4. Domus Henrici
5. Mandarin Oriental
6. Neruda
7. U Páva
8. U Raka
9. Residence Nosticova
10. Savoy
11. Zlatá Hvězda
12. U Zlaté Studné
13. U Zlatého Kola

Josefov

The Jewish Quarter lies to the north of the Royal Way and the Old Town, although little remains of what was once one of the most important Jewish communities in Central Europe. Josefov – the smallest of Prague's districts – was named after Joseph II, the Holy Roman Emperor who looked favourably on the city's Jewish community; today, tumbledown graveyards, ancient synagogues, narrow streets and gem dealers are all that remain of this once-proud area. Among the many legends of Josefov is the Golem, a figure of Jewish folklore made from inanimate matter, who used to defend the Jewish ghettoes and scare children into good behaviour.

The sophisticated shopping street of Pařížská splits the district in two, contrasting the crumbling splendour of the Jewish community with the elegance of the modern designer retailers. This is Prague's equivalent of London's Sloane Street; international fashion houses have had a presence here for years, and are steadily squeezing out the tackier, more tourist-orientated stores.

The Rudolfinium, home of the Czech Philharmonic Orchestra, presides over náměstí Jana Palacha. This open square is named after a 21-

year-old who set himself alight in protest at the Soviet invasion; in a show of solidarity over 800,000 people attended his funeral. Close by stands the Museum of Decorative Arts, which displays the kind of innovative Art Deco and Art Nouveau pieces and fine glassware for which the city is so renowned.

East of Pařížská is where Prague's more urbane nightlife is found; the cocktail bars Bugsy's, Tretters and Ocean Drive form a social nucleus all of their own, where the city's affluent locals and ex-pats can congregate with well-heeled tourists; all these places can all get fairly lively at weekends. A more alternative scene flourishes in bars such as the Tom Tom Club and the Roxy nightclub.

Overall, Josefov is a fascinating and pleasant district; like its neighbouring quarters, its narrow lanes and plethora of sights, cafés, shops and bars make it perfect for exploring on foot.

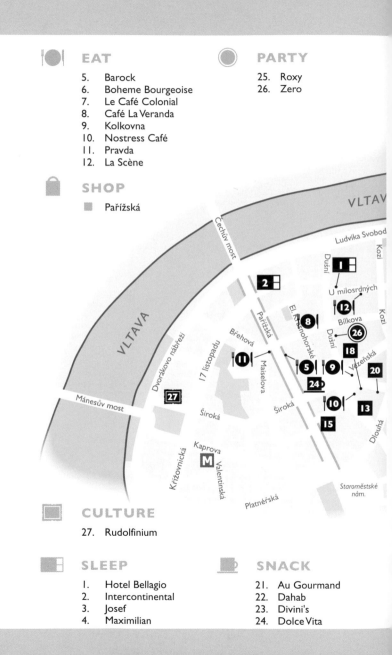

EAT

5. Barock
6. Boheme Bourgeoise
7. Le Café Colonial
8. Café La Veranda
9. Kolkovna
10. Nostress Café
11. Pravda
12. La Scène

SHOP

■ Pařížská

PARTY

25. Roxy
26. Zero

CULTURE

27. Rudolfinium

SLEEP

1. Hotel Bellagio
2. Intercontinental
3. Josef
4. Maximilian

SNACK

21. Au Gourmand
22. Dahab
23. Divini's
24. Dolce Vita

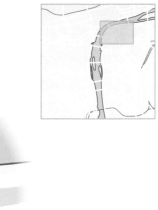

0   125   250m

M Metro Station

DRINK

13. Alcohol Bar
14. Bombay Cocktail Bar
15. Bugsy's
16. Kozicka
17. M1
18. Ocean Drive
19. Tom Tom Club
20. Tretters

sleep...

The surge in tourism that accompanied the collapse of the claustrophobic Communist era provoked a corresponding upswing in the standard and range of Prague's accommodation. By the early 1990s, buildings in the city centre were being transformed into hotels; many were developed from grand old town houses, others born from the refurbishments of existing hotels.

Hotels in the centre of Prague have never been of any real size; most offerings have been developed within one or two adjoining townhouses, creating intimate little spaces spaces with only a handful of bedrooms and few facilities.

Within a few years the established hotel brands had arrived, bringing a new level of class and convenience to tourists and business travellers alike; but the most exciting trend has surely been the recent growth of the luxury and boutique hotel sectors, where elegant architecture is married with stylish design and top facilities. Some of the more recent additions include the modern design of the ICON hotel and the old world of glamour of the Patchuv Palace (right).

Prague today offers a full range of rooms for even the most discerning of visitors, from Art Nouveau *grandes dames* and luxury chains to intimate town

houses, pseudo-palaces and designer hideaways. Five years ago most would offer only limited service or facilities, rooms were often spartan and filled with heavy dark wooden traditional furniture. Today, WiFi is standard, hotels now incorporate excellent restaurants and even the hotel lobby bar scene, so important in New York and London, is beginning to take off.

We have tried our best not to include any anonymous chain hotels here, but in their stead the best of the boutique and design hotel scene, as well as comfortable, interesting places well suited to the business traveller or those who require a certain level of comfort and facility, such as Prague's Intercontinental, Four Seasons Prague and newly opened Mandarin Oriental (left). In 2008 Rocco Forte is set to open a new hotel continuing the trend for high profile, beautifully designed boutique hotel groups to develop grand old buildings into stylish and opulent offerings.

We've picked out what we consider to be the best of the bunch, ensuring at the same time that we cover the gamut of styles, locations and price ranges.

Prices quoted below are the rack rates per room per night, and range from the cost of a double in low season to a suite in high season. High season runs from the beginning of April through to the end of October, and also includes Christmas and New Year. If you head to our website www.hg2.com you will be able to find cheaper rates and extra treats when you book your hotel room through us.

Our top 10 places to stay in Prague are:
1. Carlo IV
2. Mandarin Oriental
3. Aria
4. Four Seasons
5. Pachtuv Palace
6. Alchymist Grand Hotel & Spa
7. Josef
8. Iron Gate
9. Neruda
10. ICON

Our top 5 for style are:
1. Carlo IV
2. Aria
3. Alchymist Grand Hotel & Spa
4. Josef
5. 987

Our top 5 for atmosphere are:
1. Four Seasons
2. U Prince
3. Mandarin Oriental
4. Iron Gate
5. Pachtuv Palace

Our top 5 for location are:
1. Aria
2. Mandarin Oriental
3. Pachtuv Palace
4. Carlo IV
5. Alchymist Grand Hotel & Spa

987 Prague, Senovážné Náměstí 15, Nové Město
Tel: 255 737 100   www.designhotelscollection.com
Rates: 4,250–9,650kc

987 is one of the newer spots in Prague, and goes some way towards representing the new designer face of the city's accommodation scene. Located in
a quiet area at the edge of the city centre (a 10-minute stroll will take you

to Wenceslas Square), this hotel is unapologetically trendy. Spread over five
floors, 987 has 80 rooms – all lovingly manicured with natty orange lights
glowing gently outside, flat screens, rain showers and smart, modern furnishings inside. While some boutique hotels are cool to the point of glacial,
987's warmth is immediately apparent thanks to friendly staff, an inviting
decorative style – and, of course, the wonderful fireplace in the pleasant
reception lounge. That first impression is carried with you into the orange
glass lift that whooshes you up to your reasonably sized and impeccably
clean room. While the hotel offers a rather swish meeting room for business travellers, it's worth being aware that there's no real restaurant (just a
snazzy snack bar, where breakfast is served), gym or fitness centre.

Style 8, Atmosphere 8, Location 8

Alchymist Grand, Tržiště 19, Malá Strana
Tel: 257 286 011   www.alchymisthotel.com
Rates: 8,500–31,000kc

Since opening in 2006, the Alchymist has made a sizeable and sustained impression on the Prague hotel scene. Located within a baroque landmark (formerly U Jesizek Palace), the hotel was never going to be accused of understatement, although few perhaps realized how ambitious the management's plans were. As soon as you step past the small, stuccoed café and into the royal foyer, with its vaulted ceilings, sumptuous furnishings and exquisitely restored hallways, you know you're in special territory. The great

news is that the hotel maintains the opulent theme throughout; rooms feature regal red and gold chairs and desks, wooden marble bathrooms and period paintings, as well as modern concessions such as air-conditioning, plasma TVs, DVD/CD players and high-speed internet. They're a good size, too – particularly the suites, which are palatial. Add to this a decent restaurant, extremely good service and a heavenly spa in the basement and you have one seriously classy – not to mention romantic – hotel.

Style 10, Atmosphere 9, Location 9

Andel's, Stroupežnického 21, Smíchov
Tel: 296 889 688 www.andelshotel.com
Rates: 7,440–10,230kc

 Andels was one of Prague's first and most considered responses to the designer hotel revolution, commissioned by the Vienna International group (owners of other upmarket Prague hotels such as the Palace, Le Palais and the Savoy) and opened in 2002. It was built to form part of Smichov's commercial centre, and the artistic force behind the hotel are Jestico and Whiles

– the architect and design company responsible for London's The Hempel and One Aldwych. 'Andel' is the Czech word for 'angel' and, sure enough, the hotel favours bright, white, linear spaces (with thematic splashes of red), enhanced by a pale limestone lobby floor and reception desk, white walls and translucent curtains. The hotel's lower levels, which house the reception, bar, restaurant and conference facilities, are primarily built from glass, allowing fine views over the city. The 239 rooms and exclusive serviced studios and apartments have natural wooden features and Italian furnishings, and come equipped with DVD players, air-conditioning, internet access and slick glass bathrooms. The bar and restaurant are very good too – a necessity since the surrounding area isn't exactly brimming with facilities (although you can find both a shopping centre and multiplex cinema nearby).

Style 9, Atmosphere 8, Location 7

Aria Hotel, Tržiště 9, Malá Strana
Tel: 225 334 111   www.aria.cz
Rates: 6,700–34,200kc

One of Prague's most individual hotels, the musically themed Aria was created by Czech hotel entrepreneur Henry Kallan as a complement to his more bookish Library Hotel in New York. Each of the four floors is dedicated to a different musical genre (jazz, opera, classical, contemporary), and the 52 rooms represent an additional musical period or persona, covering everything from Rossini to Brahms and The Beatles. The theme is raised beyond novelty by an array of other delightful touches: the sweeping floor mosaic that ushers guests into the magnificent lobby; carpets embroidered with musical notes; a cosy Music Salon (with fireplace); plus a Music Box room (which shows music-themed movies on a large plasma screen), a 1000-plus library of CDs, and a staff musicologist

who can guide you through your composer's oeuvre, as well as recommend concerts and events in the city during your stay. The rooms and public areas have been painstakingly styled by Italian architect–designer Rocco Magnoli (best known for creating Versace's boutiques), while Czech artist Joseph Blecha has adorned the rooms with caricatures of musical legends. The rooms, all large, feature flat-screen computers with downloaded music, huge beds, DVD players and Molton Brown bath products. This is accommodation of the highest quality, beguilingly beautiful, charming and well thought out. If you can't afford to stay here, at least pop in for a drink on a sunny day to admire the stunning terrace views from the rooftop café.

Style 9, Atmosphere 9, Location 9

Carlo IV, Senovážné náměstí 13, Nové Město
Tel: 224 593 111 www.boscolohotels.com
Rates: 8,050–32,100kc

Opulent is an understatement for the Boscoli family's Carlo IV. Conceived and created with the talents of celebrated hotel and restaurant designer Adam Tihany and Italian architect Maurizio Papiri, this extravagant hotel opened in 2003 after a three-year, multi-million pound redevelopment. Located in a former post office and bank that dates from 1890, the space embellishes the parts of the original infrastructure that were left intact with immaculate design ideas that carry a conspicuously Italian twist. Wide steps at the entrance lead into a stunning rectangular reception and rooms that brim with subtle fusion touches such as vaulted ceilings and frescoes with gold leaf and slick glass. The rooms are tastefully decorated in beiges, browns and whites, with modern décor featured alongside 19th-century

desks or beds. Some of the public spaces betray hidden virtuosity: the Box Block restaurant (a traditional Bohemian and international menu) is fiercely geometric, as is the Inn Ox Bar (see Drink), a striking retro-futuristic space furnished in alabaster and nickel. There is also a spa with a swimming pool, sauna and steam room, making this pretty much a perfect all-round option for those who like to wallow in luxury.

Style 10, Atmosphere 9, Location 9

Černý Slon, Týnská 1, Staré Město
Tel: 222 321 521   www.hotelcernyslon.cz
Rates: 2,200–5,700kc

Cerny Slon ('Black Elephant') is a small hotel situated behind the Tyn Church, just yards from Old Town Square. There are 16 rooms (35 beds in total), all furnished in a traditional, clean and simple manner. The townhouse that accommodates the hotel dates back to the 14th century and proudly bears a UNESCO heritage listing. Although it has been comprehensively renovated in the last couple of years, Cerny Slon offers an authentically historic ambience, complemented by the friendliness of the staff and owners. Suffice to say that nothing happens in too much of a hurry, even though everything is well run. There's a decent restaurant, café and wine bar on the premises, but the hotel's main appeal lies in its location within the medieval Ungelt area (built by Charles IV). Cerny Slon is perfect for those seeking a conven-

ient location, simple, quiet rooms and an affable environment.

Style 8, Atmosphere 8, Location 9

U Červené Boty, Karlova 5, Staré Město
Tel: 222 221 051
Rates: 3,900–5,300kc

U Cervené Boty ('The Red Shoe') is a tiny pension with just four suites, located slap bang on the section of the Royal Way that runs from the Old Town Square to the Castle. Built in the 17th century and renovated in 1996,

this charming guesthouse offers bedrooms containing antique furniture and heavy wooden beds, and bathrooms that are fresh, clean and modern. The owners have done as much as they can to preserve the original feel of the building, although there are plenty of modern features (including satellite

TV). The suites are spacious and reasonably bright, but be aware that those overlooking the street tend to get noisy quite early in the morning because of the rousing of the indefatigable tourist hordes. Down in the historic cellars of the hotel there's a stylish wine bar that seats 35 and offers a decent range of wines. U Cervené Boty is a great little place to stay, and very good value for what and where it is.

Style 7, Atmosphere 8, Location 9

Domus Balthasar, Mostecká 5, Malá Strana
Tel. 257 199 199 www.domus-balthasar.cz
Rates: 3,040–6,400kc

The younger sibling of the Hidden Places duo in Prague, Balthasar adopts a more stylish, design-led stance than its bigger brother, Domus Henrici. Situated in a baroque building whose foundations date back to the 14th

century, it has eight rooms that nevertheless reflect a modern, fresh approach to design: simple white walls and linen contrast with dark wooden furniture and simple pine floors; each room is also  equipped with state-of-the-art televisions, DVD players and kitchenettes. While there are no public spaces or lounges in the hotel, a café downstairs does serve tasty breakfasts, and since you're situated just a few steps from Charles Bridge, the location is unbeatable. The corner deluxe doubles offer interesting views towards the bridge and its flanking tower, and guests in all rooms get a 'personal' phone number that allows people to call them without going through reception. This is a good choice for those seeking an intimate experience without the fuss of larger hotels.

Style 8, Atmosphere 7, Location 8

Domus Henrici, Loretánská 11, Hradčany

Tel: 220 511 369 www.domus-henrici.cz

Rates: 3,040–6,400kc

Close to the Castle and discreetly positioned between its main gate, the Loreta Chapel and Strahov Monastery, this quiet backstreet residence boasts eight double rooms set in a charming period house. The building itself dates back to the 14th century (the name is that of one of the original owners), and in the 17th century it was bought by Emperor Rudolf II to

form part of the head offices of the Imperial Court. The rooms and terraces have panoramic views over the city and the Petrin gardens below. The rooms have different detailing but all are spacious and light, and offer sparse but reasonably elegant furnishings with levels of comfort one would expect from a modern hotel. The area, although central, is close to the top of Castle Hill, which can mean a bit of a schlep home at the end of each day. The walk is worthwhile for those who can manage it, but if you're not a fan of uphill jaunts or don't want to spend money on taxi rides, it's perhaps best to stay on the other side of the river. Staff can be indifferent, but the hotel does have a driver who can pick you up at the railway station or airport and can also provide private driving tours.

Style 8, Atmosphere 7, Location 7

Elite, Ostrovni 32, Nové Město

Tel: 224 932 250 www.hotelelite.cz

Rates: 3,800–6,500kc

One of the few hotels in the trendy SoNa area of Prague, Elite was renovated and reopened in 2000, although the original building dates back more than 500 years. Today it's a charming place set in a lively and interesting part of town that eschews the prevalent SoNa accent of modern and contemporary for a more traditional voice that soothes with easy-going affability. The

hotel works with many of its original features – ornate stuccowork, painted ceilings and simple beams – and is kitted out with correspondingly heavyweight wooden furniture. There are 77 uniquely decorated rooms, all containing pieces of original antique furniture, engravings of 17th-century Prague and private bathrooms. Modern features also grace the rooms, including pay TV, satellite, PC connections, WiFi and minibars; business travellers may want to request one of the rooms with a writing desk. The two main suites are spacious, and one of them comes with a 17th-century Renaissance ceiling. A courtyard provides a great summer breakfast area as well as an ambient, tranquil location for an evening drink, and the hotel is also connected to Ultramarin (see Drink) – a lively bar, restaurant and nightclub accessed through a separate entrance down the street.

Style 7, Atmosphere 8, Location 7

Esplanade, Washingtova 1600/19, Nové Město
Tel: 224 501 111 www.esplanade.cz
Rates: 3,069–12,369kc

Esplanade is a large and attractive Art Nouveau hotel at the southern end of Wenceslas Square, located close to the State Opera. Constructed during the First Republic, the hotel began life as a bank and the offices of an Italian insurance company back in the 1920s. It now has 74 elegant and comfortable rooms filled with reproduction furniture (although the chandelier in the

atrium is original). The grand appearance extends to the rooms, which are all different (in size, style and even quality – make sure you get to look at a couple if you can) and each individually furnished in early 20th-century manner, some with large oil paintings and embossed wall coverings, others with French Provincial headboards and tables. The smart lobby café and restaurant are reminiscent of the old-world splendour typical of Prague, although the sizeable conference facilities may mean you share your romantic weekend away with squadrons of corporate folk. The Esplanade is, of course, very well located for opera buffs.

Style 7, Atmosphere 7, Location 8

Floor Hotel, Na Příkope 13, Staré Město
Tel: 234 076 300 www.floorhotel.cz
Rates: 3,947–7,331kc

Yet another example of Prague's blazing boutique scene, the Floor Hotel is a smart, four-star offering occupying a very good location between Wenceslas Square and the Old Town. The funky white reception gives way to designer rooms that are generally smart and comfortable. If you score the right one you'll get plenty of space, decent furnishings and even a jacuzzi, but be aware that some of the others don't reflect the prices so well. Similarly the breakfasts, despite the surprise appearance of porridge on the menu, can fail to

live up to the promises of the good-looking breakfast room; and you'd be better off eating somewhere other than the slightly sterile El Gaucho restaurant. It ought to be mentioned also that the staff can be frustratingly nonchalant and ineffective. So why have we included it? Because even if the overriding impression is mostly of a place ironing out its flaws and finding its feet, when the Floor does get things right, it can be a very memorable place to stay.

Style 7, Atmosphere 7, Location 9

Four Seasons, Veleslavínova 2a, Staré Město
Tel: 221 427 000 www.fourseasons.com
Rates: 8,680 84,000kc

Almost immediately after opening in early 2001, the Four Seasons was forced to close for a year because of the 2002 floods. However, the hotel has now reopened as luxurious as ever, displaying all the extravagance you would expect from this exclusive brand. With fantastic views of the Castle and Charles Bridge from its privileged setting on the banks of the Vltava, the Four Seasons comprises three historic buildings from the city's most important architectural periods – Baroque, Renaissance, and Art Nouveau. The vast space houses 161 rooms and suites. All are fitted with fine wooden furniture, and some have antiques while others are more avant-garde, but conveniences from CD players to high-speed internet connections are provided in all rooms. While only some offer great views, the best suites do have balconies, sweeping vistas and sunken marble tubs. The Four Seasons is also

41

home to Allegro (see Eat), one of the city's best restaurants. Indeed, one of the highlights of a stay here is taking in dinner on the terrace of the Allegro restaurant on a balmy summer evening, followed by a symphony at the nearby Rudolfinum.

Style 9, Atmosphere 8, Location 10

Hotel Bellagio, U Milosrdných 2, Josefov
Tel: 221 778 999 www.bellagiohotel.cz
Rates: 3,380–8,000kc

Hotel Bellagio is an instantly likeable place. Located on a quiet corner of Josefov, it exudes effortless Italian chic from the moment the doorman gently ushers you into the snug lounge. There are just 46 rooms (all recently refurbished), which reflect the intimate ambience of the space, and although

they aren't the biggest you'll ever see, they are fully kitted out with import-ed Italian furniture, WiFi and LCD screens, and available in a variety of inter-esting shapes and sizes. The Bellagio's location is perfect: literally strolling-distance from the Spanish Synagogue and the trendy Pařížská shopping boulevard. There's a cosy basement Italian restaurant for romantics, a small but perfectly formed conference room (maximum capacity 30 people) for business travellers, and a smart lobby bar that stays open until 11pm each night.

Style 8, Atmosphere 8, Location 8

ICON Hotel, V Jámě 6, Nové Město
Tel: 221 634 100 www.iconhotel.eu
Rates: 6,885–7,500kc

The Mediterranean eatery Jet Set (of the same owner) and new Thai spa, Zen Asian Wellbeing flank the subtle entrance to the new ICON hotel which opens into a sunny, industrial chic lobby cum lounge with electric,

colourful furniture, concrete walls, aluminium air ducts, DJ booth and atri-um. The Diesel-clad staff and Apple computers point to canny partnerships and as the girls escort you to your room, ICON's personal touch comes forward. A forgotten Jindřich Halabala chair has been resurrected, the 31 rooms are in subdued corridors but rooms are bright, spacious, lined with tactile surfaces and loaded with ultra mod cons including, thumb-print accessed safe, ipod/mp3 port connected to the flat screen TV and DVD player. Free WiFi (in public areas) and dataport in room, wireless Skype phone, delightfully comfortable Hastens beds, slate bathrooms with Rituals products might mean you never leave your room, but the all day a la carte breakfast will fuel even the most hedonistic guest. A 1930s building has been redesigned with explicit care to provide a truly contemporary new hotel.

Style 8, Atmosphere, 8, Location 10

Intercontinental, Náměstí Curieových 5, Josefov
Tel: 296 631 111 www.ichotelsgroup.com
Rates: 8,370–12,100kc

Prague's Intercontinental was built in the 1970s, during the period of Soviet Occupation. The hotel's suites have hosted luminaries such as Michael Jackson, Madeleine Albright and – legend has it – terrorist Carlos the Jackal. Badly damaged in the 2002 floods, the Intercontinental is today back in full swing, flaunting its position at the top of fashionable Pařížská and attracting affluent business and leisure travellers who seek upmarket chain hotel facili-

ties and proximity to stylish boutiques and chic restaurants. The original 1970s design has been updated with modern rooms, a glittering, state-of-the-art fitness centre and an atrium restaurant. The standard guest rooms may not be very large but are comfortable, and feature decent but not exceptional upholstered furniture, computer ports and marble bathrooms. The hotel comes equipped with all the conveniences you'd expect, and the fitness centre includes an impressive golf simulator on which execs can play the Belfry or Augusta in between conferences. On the roof, the Zlatá Praha restaurant offers guests a scenic dining experience with views of many of

Prague's 'thousand spires'. While stylish and well equipped, the Intercontinental does not quite manage to shake off the air of a chain hotel, and those seeking a more seductive ambience should look elsewhere.

Style 7, Atmosphere 7, Location 8

Iron Gate, Michalská 19, Staré Město
Tel.: 225 777 777 www.irongate.cz
Rates: 6,200–29,760kc

The Iron Gate is set within a central courtyard that provides a short cut between Old Town Square and Wenceslas Square. This 14th century building offers a rarefied combination of residential and commercial accommodation. Currently the only member of the Preferred Hotel Group in the Czech Republic, it boasts 43 rooms (some duplex) bedecked with antique furniture, discreet kitchenettes, Italian designer cosmetics in the bathrooms and, more often than not, a built-in jacuzzi. Given the age of the building and the sensitive restoration process, there is real history on offer here – although, of course, you pay for it. Choosing a room with a restored fresco, piece of origi-nal wall or painted ceiling from the 14th–16th centuries will immediately put you into the

higher price category, but the many features in the public areas are free to marvel at. The rooms have the feel of a sophisticated apartment, although standard hotel services are always on hand. The unfeasibly charming three-floor Tower Suite (with an extra-large jacuzzi and stunning views over the rooftops of Prague) is a boon for honeymooners and romantics, as is the hotel's prime central position.

Style 9, Atmosphere 9, Location 9

Jalta, Václavské Náměstí 45, Nové Mesto

Tel: 222 822 111   www.hoteljalta.cz
Rates: 4505–10,137kc

This shining example of Czech social-realist architecture goes back to 1958, and has since been designated a cultural monument. What was once a fairly nondescript, dowdy hotel has recently been perked up into something altogether smarter, funkier and infinitely more charming. Optimistically reclaiming itself as a boutique hotel, Jalta is actually, beyond the modern lobby (with its unimaginative Kafka portrait), a fairly considered mix of old and new. The marble floors, winding staircase and wonderfully wide Art Deco corridors

are all original, but the rooms have been dolled up with boutique fabrics, modern lamps and neutral mauves, browns and creams to give them a lighter, designer feel. The front rooms over the square are necessarily fitted with double-glazed windows, but there are quieter rooms at the back. The hotel houses a couple of immense conference spaces, below which is located the hotel's super-slick restaurant, Hot (see Eat). Semi-chic without the pretension, or corporate with a modern twist: whichever way you look at it, Jalta presents a solid option right in the heart of the city.

Style 7, Atmosphere 7, Location 9/10

Josef, Rybná 20, Josefov

Tel: 221 700 111   www.hoteljosef.com
Rates: 5,344–9,472kc

A member of the Design Hotels group, the Josef boasts the distinction of being the first truly designer hotel in the Czech Republic. Even more impressive is the fact that it is still today regarded as one of the best. Created by well-known Czech architect Eva Jiřičná, the space is the epitome

of cool – a fine example of elegantly executed conceptual minimalism. To enter the glass-fronted reception is to set foot in a brave new world, comprising pristine white spaces, aluminium and chrome and spectacular touches such as glass-walled bathrooms and racy staircases. Located on a calm street close to Old Town Square, Josef also boasts a rooftop gym, grassy courtyard with patio seating for the summer, and a large modern bar and café (no restaurant), the latter of which makes a stylish location for a mid-morning coffee or early evening cocktail. The rooms, despite their inevitably funky touches, are surprisingly comfortable, and kitted out with all mod-cons (free internet connection, DVD player, etc). It comes as no surprise that the place has become the hotel of choice for rock stars, celebrities and – since it sponsors the Prague Writers' Festival – the literati too. Room no. 801, a penthouse with a magnificent vista of the Prague skyline, is highly sought after by those who want to absorb the golden city in its full glory.

Style 9, Atmosphere 8, Location 9

K + K Hotel Central, Hybernská 10, Nové Město
Tel: 225 022 000 www.kkhotels.cz
Rates: 7,775–9,050kc

The new sister hotel to the Fenix (see below), the Central has been constructed as a flagship venue for the entire K + K chain. The building was a

hotel (of the same name) back in the 19th century, before it was transformed into a theatre in the 1920s and a cinema in the 1930s. Designer Alison Clarke has maintained many of the original Art Nouveau features, fusing them with stark modern touches such as the eye-catching glass and perspex multifunction cube that commands the main hall, and which houses a conference room below and a breakfast room on top. Rooms are geared towards corporate and leisure travellers, with comfortable, linear furnishings, free internet, LCD screens and – in the older part of the building – lovely high ceilings (the rooms in the new section have pleasant views onto a garden area). The wonderful stairs and lift retain their original look, contrasting with the swish neon bar, and don't miss the roofless sauna in the health club, where you can lie down and gaze at the marvellous cupola above.

Style 8, Atmosphere 8, Location 8

K + K Hotel Fenix, Ve Smečkách 30, Nové Město
Tel: 233 092 222 www.kkhotels.com
Rates: 7,575–8,850kc

Hotel Fenix, situated on a side street running off Wenceslas Square, possesses a surprising amount of flair. To all intents and purposes it's a chain hotel, but the light, airy lobby creates a great first impression that extends, more or less, throughout the rest of the building. Popular with business travellers as well as a younger leisure crowd, it mixes interior design and state-of-the-art amenities and seems to attract a decent range of clientele. Fenix has 130 rooms in total, most of them decorated with muted colours and modern furniture. Front windows are double-glazed, which is just as well since the hotel is unfortunately (or fortunately, depending on your point of view) close to two of the town's best known adult clubs: Atlas and Darling (see Party). The rooms at the back are quieter, and it's just a short walk from here to the centre of the city and away from the hubbub outside. With a health club in the basement and a business centre just off the lobby, this is a good all-round option.

Style 7, Atmosphere 7, Location 8

Mandarin Oriental, Nebovidská 459/1, Malá Strana

Tel: 233 088 888   www.mandarinoriental.com
Rates: 7,600–113,100kc

While every other hotel in Prague occupies an ancient house, palace or public building, not many inhabit the former ruins of a 14th-century monastery. The Mandarin Oriental thus offers something rather special, even

by this city's increasingly sky-high standards. The monastery's ancient features have inevitably been incorporated into the hotel design, most notably down in the spa where the remains of a Gothic church are laid out below a glass floor, and in the fitness centre, which houses a section of a medieval bridge. But the modern is very much in evidence too. Juxtaposed with the vaulted ceilings, 172-square-metre ballroom and parquet floors is an uberswanky bar, a sublime restaurant (Essensia; see Eat) and 99 rooms that are surprisingly understated but extremely refined. Both the rooms and suites brim with subtle Eastern touches, sumptuous textiles and handcrafted finishes, and boast limestone bathrooms with heated floors as well as built-in LCD TVs. The presidential suite is to die for, and the spa is one of the city's best (see Play).

Style 9, Atmosphere 9, Location 9

Maximilian, Haštalská 14, Josefov

Tel: 225 303 111 www.maximilianhotel.com
Rates: 2,823–10,933kc

The Maximilian aims for the same kind of comfort and style as its sister hotel, the Josef (see page 46), but adopts a slightly less self-conscious air – think Small Luxury rather than Design Hotel. Reconstructed throughout 2005, the hotel offers 70 rooms and one suite. Josef designer Eva Jiřičná has worked the Maximilian into a sweeping amalgamation of Art Deco, Modernism and contemporary design styles. A colourful library, snug drawing room (with fireplace) and glass-roofed breakfast section provide com-

fortable public spaces. The guest rooms are similarly inviting with their
Eileen Grey tables, swooshes of blue and orange across neutral colour
schemes and a range of conveniences (rain showers, telephones, ISDN/WiFi,
satellite TV). The emphasis is very much on personal service here, and with
a dedicated Sabai spa downstairs (complete with therapy rooms, flotation
centre and Thai massage), the Maximilian is a great place to unwind.

Style 8, Atmosphere 8, Location 8

Neruda, Nerudova 44, Malá Strana
Tel: 257 535 557 www.hotel-neruda.cz
Rates: 5,760–7,050kc

Set just beneath the Castle on the busy and winding street of Nerudova, in
the Malá Strana district, Neruda is named (like the street) after Czech
writer and poet Jan Neruda. Neruda documented Malá Strana obsessively in
his work, and quotations adorn the hotel walls. Ranking among the most
stylish hotels in the city, Neruda's original villa dates from the 14th century.
As such, the hotel embodies a comfortable meld of straight-up modernism

and modest classicism. The ground-floor entrance lobby, café and lounge set
the tone for the rest of the building: clean lines, simple materials (glass,
stone, aluminium, granite) and designer furniture – motifs that are repeated
particularly throughout the hotel's 20 crisp, contemporary rooms, each neu-
trally decorated and featuring light, modern bathrooms. The hotel is
equipped with all the facilities expected of a first-rate spot (air-conditioning,
satellite TV, etc.), and with 23 new rooms soon to be opened in an addition-

al adjacent building (designed by local architect and glass artist Bořek Šípek), there will soon be even more opportunity to experience the natural tranquillity of this popular spot.

Style 8, Atmosphere 9, Location 8

Pachtuv Palác, Karolíny Světlé 34, Staré Město
Tel: 234 705 111   www.pachtuvpalace.com
Rates: 10,000–20,500kc

Looking for a mix of authentic Prague history and upmarket luxury? The Pachtuv Palace, once a genuine palace owned by the Pachta family, could be a sterling option. The front of the building dates back 150 years, while other sections are twice as old. Situated at the end of Karolíny Světlé, just steps away from Charles Bridge and directly opposite the wonderful Bellevue

restaurant (see Eat), this MaMaison property offers 50 apartments/rooms and an interior designed by Jane Wilson (of London's Dorchester fame). The place exudes a regal aura, echoed by antique wooden beams, frescos, vaulted chapel ceilings, sculptures and original fireplaces. The apartments are richly decorated with a blend of antique and modern furnishings, rugs and paintings, while the 'exceptional apartments' and honeymoon suite cater for even more refined/expensive tastes. The location is a key selling-point, as is the gorgeous summer garden, and the fact that Mozart stayed here (he was apparently locked in a room by the owner until he finished a promised concerto). Note that while the deluxe rooms have river views, the rear rooms are older and more remote.

Style 9, Atmosphere 9, Location 10

Palace, Panská 12, Nové Město
Tel: 224 093 111 www.palacehotel.cz
Rates: 4,000–10,750kc

One of the smartest hotels in Prague, the appositely titled Palace was first
opened in 1909. Today it forms part of the Vienna International Hotels
group, but still offers the kind of style and pomp you'd expect from an old-
world hotel. After all, there must

be a reason why Enrico Caruso,
Steven Spielberg and Prince
Charles chose to stay here.
Signs of continuing grandeur are
happily ubiquitous, most notably
in the lobby and the façade of
the hotel. There is a good
restaurant and a decent bar
attached, and service throughout is impeccable. The one-time
glory of the rooms has faded
somewhat, replaced by a comfortable and functional aesthetic
that panders to business and
leisure travellers alike. That said,
the Italian white marble bathrooms with extra telephones
are a nice touch, and recent

refurbishments have made the rooms more up to date and relieved them of
some of their former stuffiness. The hotel is popular not only with visiting
dignitaries and the odd celebrity but also with high-class tour groups and
conferences; still, anyone seeking an upmarket and individual experience
should feel at home here.

Style 8, Atmosphere 8, Location 8

Le Palais, U Zvonařky 1, Vinohrady
Tel: 222 563 351 www.palaishotel.cz
Rates: 5,720–51,200kc

This edifice, constructed at the end of the 19th century, was entirely renovated in 2001–02 by the Vienna International Hotels group. Located in what
was once a palace (unsurprisingly, given the name), the beautiful Belle
Époque space retains many of its original features, including wooden ceilings,
stuccowork and murals. With nods to the modern, the hotel is also

equipped with all of the necessary mod-cons, a great restaurant (Le Papillon,
run by Radek Subrt), relaxing bar and also a health spa/fitness centre.
Although it's a beautiful place to stay, it should be mentioned that Le Palais
is a 30-minute walk (or 10-minute taxi ride) from the centre. These days,
however, its location is not so much of a problem since the quiet and affluent Vinohrady neighbourhood enjoys an assortment of sophisticated bars
and restaurants. The 72 rooms, designed, like the interior, by Veronika
Jurkowitsch, are comfortable, but kitted out with slightly predictable chain-
hotel furniture and coverings. It's worth paying the extra for one of the
suites with an open fireplace if you feel like adding a splash of colour and
romance to your stay.

Style 8, Atmosphere 8, Location 6

Paříz, U Obecního domu 1, Staré Město
Tel: 222 195 195 www.hotel-paris.cz
Rates: 9,600–110,000kc

A classic Art Nouveau hotel in the centre of Prague, Paříz is probably the
most upmarket in town. Built in 1904 next to the Municipal House – another grand Art Nouveau edifice – the hotel has retained its turn-of-the-

century elegance even through subsequent renovations and modernizations. After registering in the classic secese lobby, follow the correspondingly sinuous banister up to comfortable, high-ceilinged rooms that incorporate modern furnishings with an Art Nouveau twist (soft furnishings and carpets are surprisingly anonymous), and clean, crisp bathrooms covered in French

cobalt and white tiles. If you feel like splashing out, the Royal Tower Suite is extremely luxurious; planned like a loft apartment with sympathetically designed furniture, it is capped by fabulous 360° views of the city. The restaurant, bar and lobby exude an aura of resplendent grandeur, and the hotel has all the facilities that you might expect or need, including a Wellness and Spa Centre. The restaurant, Sarah Bernhardt, offers very good cuisine, and the Cafe de Pariz is a great place for a spot of afternoon tea – which, of course, you will pay for handsomely.

Style 9, Atmosphere 8, Location 8

U Páva, U Lužického semináře, Malá Strana
Tel: 257 533 573 www.romantichotels.cz
Rates: 3,500–8,200kc

U Páva, meaning 'At the Peacock', was one of the first hotels to be renovated after the Velvet Revolution, saving the house from destruction and retaining much of its historical character. Located on a quiet street close to Charles Bridge, U Páva now offers 19 rooms and eight suites, scattered amid three buildings. It's certainly one of the most romantic hotels in the city, with some of the rooms claiming superior views of the Castle. Plentiful wooden panelling, painted ceilings, rich textiles and ornate period furniture all set the scene, while a fairly stylish restaurant and café provide extra

facilities and, in the case of the latter, large leather armchairs to sink into. One of the most traditional and comfortable hotels in the city, U Páva is ideal for a romantic weekend away, and is particularly cosy — like Prague itself — in the winter months.

Style 8, Atmosphere 8, Location 9

U Prince, Staromžstské náměstí 29, Staré Město
Tel: 224 213 807   www.hoteluprince.cz
Rates: 4,190–10,990kc

One of the more original and romantic hotels in the city, U Prince is constructed in the shell of a 12th-century building. You couldn't ask for a more central location — step out the front door and you're virtually embracing the Astronomical Clock on Old Town Square. The 15 rooms, seven suites and two apartments are all fairly spacious, and furnished with heavy antique

wooden furniture and tasteful decorations that include restored painted wooden ceilings. Double-glazing protects the front rooms, which face the constant hubbub of the square. Having undergone a major refurbishment in 2001, the hotel is now equipped with a smartly arranged front terrace, seafood restaurant, wine bar and also a superlative roof terrace that offers sensational views over the city. Best of all, U Prince prides itself on providing an intimate experience, emphasizing not only upmarket tranquillity but also professional service. It's not the cheapest spot in town, but it does offer a piece of the past, an almost unsurpassed feeling of romance, and a location that couldn't be more central if it tried.

Style 8, Atmosphere 8, Location 10

Radisson SAS Alcron, Štěpánská 40, Nové Město
Tel: 222 820 000 www.radissonsas.com
Rates: 7,100–11,300kc

While we may be disinclined to rave about chain hotels, the SAS Alcron is a little more special than most. Before the Radisson group took it over, the original hotel had been a Prague institution for many years. Today it still dis-

plays a strong Art Deco influence and retains many original features – heavy crystal chandeliers, rich Italian marble and creamy 'milk glass' – enough to drive home the feeling that you couldn't be anywhere else in the world other than Prague. The 211 rooms are comfortable and designed to complement the communal areas with classic period furnishings. The Alcron's central location, just off Wenceslas Square and a 10-minute stroll from Old Town Square, puts you close to the opera houses. The clincher, however, just might be the

Alcron restaurant – one of the finest in the city, specializing in the kind of remarkable seafood dishes that make it almost worth staying here for the food alone.

Style 8, Atmosphere 7, Location 8

U Raka, Černínská 10, Hradčany
Tel: 220 511 100 www.romantikhotel-uraka.cz
Rates: 6,200–7,900kc

Hidden away in a beautiful, unspoiled section of the city (think stuccoed houses and cobblestone streets), this small, romantic hotel looks astonish-

ingly like a country farmstead, complete with wooden timbers, trickling water and various agricultural knick-knacks. Embellishing the peaceful atmosphere is the fact that there really is very little in the vicinity to distract you. Rooms are rustic, furnished in an elegant but basic manner, with wrought-iron or heavy wooden beds and country furniture with plain, muted colours. Natural materials such as wood and stone abound, giving the place a Rousseau-esque 'back to nature' feel – an ambience heightened by the small but sensitively landscaped garden areas. Popular with honeymooners and the romantically inclined, it has only one downside: the slight trek to Old Town Square and Staré Město.

Style 8, Atmosphere 8, Location 6

Residence Nosticova, Nosticova 1, Malá Strana
Tel: 257 312 513 www.nosticova.com
Rates:5,000–16,500kc

A firm favourite with Prague's film industry, this small, 10-room hotel around the corner from Charles Bridge (Malá Strana side) often becomes home to visiting actors and directors for the duration of their shoot. Each of the apartment-style suites is tradition-

ally furnished, but unlike other 'traditional' establishments, these are slightly more refined. One of the most interesting suites, the Arcimboldo (named after the famous 16th-century painter), houses the hotel's only four-poster bed and is the romantic room of choice. Standard features such as laundry and room service are available, but although there is none of the mod-cons that most other high-end hotels offer, the staff's assistance and attention to detail are effortlessly precise, leaving the impulse to relax overwhelming. On the ground floor, the newly refurbished Alchemy restaurant is a welcome boon, making this an excellent choice for families, movie aficionados or anyone wanting a slightly more independent experience.

Style 8, Atmosphere 8, Location 8

Residence Řetězová, Řetězová 9, Staré Město
Tel: 222 221 800   www.residenceretezova.com
Rates: 3,840–12,000kc

A collection of nine serviced apartments set in a town house just a few minutes from Old Town Square, whose interiors range in size from small studios to large two-bedroom flats. All are furnished in a different style and titled with the names of European capital cities, but without any decorative references to their namesakes. Many original features are still in place, such as vaulted ceilings and frescoed wooden panelling, as well original 15th-century roof frames, and each space has at least one Italian-style bath and a kitchenette with state-of-the-art cooking facilities. A concierge service can provide any meals you might need, as well as concert bookings, car hire and

even baby-sitting. Breakfast is not included but there are three very good cafés within 20 yards of the front door. The Retězová can be an interesting place to stay, has a great location and friendly staff, and is an especially good choice for families.

Style 8, Atmosphere 8, Location 9

Riverside, Janáčkovo Nábřeží 15, Smíchov
Tel: 225 994 611 www.riversideprague.com
Rates: 7,040–18,880kc

The Riverside opened in 2002 and has made an impressive inroad into Prague's designer hotel scene. A product of the French group Orco, the hotel combines modern elegance and comfort with old-fashioned Art Nouveau décor and breathtaking views. Situated on the riverbank, as the

name suggests, Riverside overlooks not just the Vlatva but also the Castle (if you get the high room on the north-facing side), as well as Frank Gehry's impressive Dancing House. Simple but stylish rooms are the product of Pascale de Montrémy's design vision, and include the comfortable Room 603, which has a stunning panorama and balcony. The standard rooms are not particularly spacious, but nor are they insufficient. A relaxed and modish lobby bar is the perfect place to sip a cocktail, making the only minus points the lack of a restaurant and a brisk 20-minute walk into the centre.

Style 8, Atmosphere 8, Location 7

Savoy, Keplerova ul. 6, Hradčany
Tel: 224 302 430   www.hotel-savoy.cz
Rates: 10,240–31,680kc

One of the city's old-guard hotels, this 55-room establishment is popular with the A-list, and often plays host to visiting football teams (in part because of its proximity to the training pitches). The hotel was reopened in

1994, and has retained its original façade and many other impressive features. Internally the space offers what one might expect from a Savoy, with rooms stuffed full of marble, modern amenities and predictably patterned carpets. A restaurant serves excellent international and Czech food, there's a pleasant Wellness Centre downstairs, and service in general is friendly bordering on obsequious. The atmosphere can feel just the wrong side of formal at times (it's popular with visiting officials), and although the location at the top of the hill and close to the Castle means there are plenty of

neighbouring attractions and more than a few restaurants, the region lacks
the vibrancy associated with other popular areas such as Old Town Square.

Style 7, Atmosphere 7, Location 7

Ungelt, Malá Štupartská 1, Staré Město
Tel: 224 828 686   www.ungelt.cz
Rates: 4,500–6,800kc

Located close to Old Town Square, this small boutique hotel doubles up as
a miniature time capsule. Different parts of the hotel hark back (via various

reconstruc-
tions) all the
way to the
12th century.
Ungelt's 10
apartments are
split into one-
and two-bed-
room options,
and come fur-
nished with a
mixture of

antique furniture and 1990s Eastern European styles. Each has its own character, as well as its own kitchen and dining facilities, and breakfast is deliv-
ered to the room each morning. For a small hotel, Ungelt doesn't scrimp on
space; the suites are large (some are very suitable for families) and display a
real sense of independence from the traditional hotel format. The only
drawbacks are the general lack of views (a few rooms at the back look onto
a pleasant courtyard, however), and the proximity of the rooms on the east
side to a popular bar, which means they can get a little noisy at times.

Style 7, Atmosphere 8, Location 9

Ventana Hotel Prague, Celetna 7, Staré Město
Tel: 221 776 600   www.ventana-hotel.net
Rates: 4,230–12,694kc

The Ventana, an 18th-century residential building, was converted into a five-star hotel and opened in August 2004. The hotel's main draw is its location, situated right on the corner of busy Celetna and dawdling distance from Old Town Square. It's an attractive space, with a floor and portico riveted

with Italian marble and a hall adorned with iron and sophisticated lighting that illuminates the high, semi-stuccoed ceilings. A slick glass-walled lift transports guests to their rooms (or the first-floor bar), ascending through the space in the middle of the original stone spiral staircase. The rooms are more comfortable than chic, although they are large and (mostly) possess unbeatable views over King's Row, Tyn Church or Old Town Square; those on the top floor (the Skyloft rooms) additionally feature mezzanine levels, antique beams and interesting layouts. The Library and Ventana Bar are also wonderful Art Deco spaces, often used for fashion shoots, with polished teak floors and large windows for daydreaming.

Style 7, Atmosphere 7, Location 9

Yasmin, Politických Věznu 12, Staré Město
Tel: 234 100 100   www.hotel-yasmin.cz
Rates: 6,200–9,587kc

Opened in March 2006, the Yasmin is one of the more prominent 'second wave' designer hotels sweeping into Prague's Old Town area. A partnership project of the Four Seasons (although conceptually distinct from the brand), the Yasmin boasts a handy location near Wenceslas Square. The perspex, lin-ear reception area, with its vivid mix of lime-green décor and orange-unformed staff, introduces you to a decidedly modern space. The Yasmin's main achievement is combining this designer flair with a very subtle corporate edge. Situated within two buildings – one mod-

ern, one historical – its 200 rooms are decorated in the hotel's pervasive olive-green (or 'Yasmin Green', as they would have it), although the bathrooms are attired with immaculate black tiles. The beds have perspex headboards and rooms feature mod-cons including LCD TVs, air conditioning and internet access. Funkier, perhaps, are the colourful conference rooms, the circular beaded-curtain lounge area, and associated restaurant, Noodles (see Snack). There's also a small fitness centre on the ground floor.

Style 8, Atmosphere 8, Location 8

Zlatá Hvězda, Nerudova 48, Hradčany
Tel: 257 532 867 www.hotelgoldenstar.com
Rates: 3,648–7,232kc

Zlatá Hvězda ('Golden Star'), an imposing building with 24 rooms and two apartments, sits at the top of Nerudova on the way up to the Castle. In the 14th century it belonged to the mayor of Prague, and after passing through many private ownerships, opened to the public in May 2000. Original architectural features remain intact and the design of the hotel has highlighted many of the key aspects of the space while managing to incorporate a modern standard of comfort. The rooms are very relaxing and the reproduction furniture combines well with the architecture, helped along by an ethic of simple wooden floors and light walls. A sizeable restaurant on the ground floor (with a terrace situated on the street) affords views of the tourist-filled but nonetheless picturesque area. Although its charm and affability are

not in question, the location up the hill might be a hike too far for some.

Style 8, Atmosphere 8, Location 8

U Zlaté Studně, U Zlaté Studně 4, Malá Strana
Tel: 257 533 322 www.zlatestudne.cz
Rates: 5,150–9,900kc

Situated a statue's throw from Charles Bridge and the British Embassy, this 16th-century Renaissance building (once home to the famous metal-nosed astronomer Tycho Brahe) was renovated a short time ago to create 17 attractive rooms and three plush suites. Everything has been refurbished to a high standard, with a plethora of reproduction furniture spread throughout. Each room contains a whirlpool bath and heated bathroom floors, but

it's the spectacular views over most of the Old Town and stretching away up to Žižkov that steal the show. U Zlaté Studně ('The Golden Well') also has an eponymous

restaurant on the top floor – open to the public – with an outside terrace that also enjoys the panorama, as well as serving up top-class food (see Eat). The hotel is central but still, nestled in quiet surroundings, set at the end of a small alley beyond the traffic routes; your only distraction comes from the gentle pitter-patter of the fountains situated in the hotel's gardens below.

Style 8, Atmosphere 9, Location 9

U Zlatého Kola, Nerudova 28, Hradčany
Tel: 257 535 490 www.thegoldenwheel.com
Rates: 5,120–8,320kc

Nestled at the base of the Castle walls on Nerudova street (part of the Royal Way), U Zlatého Kola lends a sense of substance and style to the area, much like its neighbour, the Neruda. With only 17 rooms behind its impressive baroque façade, U Zlatého Kola takes a gourmet rather than gourmand approach to space, ensuring that this town house exudes a decent aura of room and privacy. The interior is a successful amalgamation of modern and traditional styles, where fresh designer furnishings work with traditional painted ceilings. Rooms boast contemporary bedrooms, resplendent with arty photographs and  impressive black-and-white tiled bathrooms; the space of the upper floors looks out towards the Castle walls and St Vitus' Cathedral, or across to the Petřin tower and surrounding park. Other hidden charms include a garden at the top of the house, a glass balcony look-out point and a glass box lift. The stylish little café downstairs, Arcadia, sells ridiculously rich hot chocolates and proper Italian coffee. U Zlatého Kola is clearly a boutique hotel worthy of the title.

Style 8, Atmosphere 8, Location 8

Notes & Updates

eat...

Once upon a time, Bohemian food was right up with the best in Europe. At the beginning of the 19th century, the region's gastronomy was considered equal to that of France, Italy and Britain. The events of the last hundred years or so put paid to that, but – curmudgeonly Communist eras notwithstanding – the country has managed to survive with some of its older culinary traditions intact.

In Prague especially, things have come a long way since the lacklustre efforts of the 1980s. The city now hosts a wide range of restaurants, offering a full variety of dining options, from traditional Czech food to French, Italian and other international options, including vegetarian fare. Fusion dishes and conventional classics can appear side by side on the same menu, and prices can be just as diverse – you can eat reasonably cheaply or splurge out on a delectable meal to be remembered.

To experience some local flavour, you can do no better than order a traditional Czech meal. Popular dishes include, but are not restricted to, wild boar, duck, carp or perch, red cabbage and dumplings, and sauces rich in cream and butter. Combine these kinds of ingredients with over-generous portions and it may well be that your arteries will be screaming for relief before you've finished your trip.

Much Czech cuisine on offer in beer halls and the more tourist-based restaurants will often be over-cooked, over-salted and over-proportioned; on the plus side it'll fill you up, which is great if you are out walking all day, haven't eaten in an aeon, or plan to spend a late night in one of the city's many clubs. Modern Czech cooking, on the other hand, is based on the same rich meats but uses more refined cooking methods and delicate sauces.

One of the best spots to try traditional dishes is Kolkovna, part of the Czech-owned chain of the same name. Even if the food isn't world class, the ambience is reasonably authentic. One of the more upper-class options, offering unique takes on century-old classics, is Boheme Bourgeoise (below).

If Czech food doesn't float your boat, you will find plenty of other options listed below. Italian trattorias, French bistros, Moroccan tearooms, Thai eateries,
sushi bars…whatever you're craving, you'll be able to find it here. Many international restaurants also offer traditional Czech food, so you can leave these difficult decisions until the very last minute. The Czech dining experience seems to
be changing by the year. Czechs are now eating much more fish, beef and even
vegetarian meals. The discerning veggie diner will enjoy places such as the funky
Lehka Hlava.

The ratings awarded in this section result from our first-hand experience of all
the restaurants recommended here. Points for food are awarded for quality,
choice and presentation. With regard to service, efficiency, speed and courte-
ousness are paramount. We judge a restaurant's atmosphere according to its
style, the friendliness of its staff, how busy it is and its general ambience. The
price given for each restaurant is based on the cost of an average two-course
meal for one, with half a bottle of wine, including service and local taxes.

When tipping, 10% is the absolute minimum. Also good to remember is that
many places – but not all – offer non-smoking sections. For more popular
restaurants, reservations are a must – particularly if you're looking for 'elite'
seats on the terrace or tables along the river in the more touristy areas. It's
merely a matter of time before the cuisine of Prague matches its spectacular
architecture. Enjoy trusting in the refreshingly classic choices the city has on
offer, but don't be afraid to try something deliciously new…

Our top 10 restaurants in Prague are:
1. Kampa Park
2. Allegro
3. V Zátiší
4. Boheme Bourgeoise
5. Essensia
6. Hergetova Cihelná
7. Alcron
8. Atelier
9. Rybí Trh
10. La Perle de Prague

Our top five for food are:
1. Allegro
2. Kampa Park
3. Boheme Bourgeoise
4. Essensia
5. V Zátiší

Our top five for service are:
1. Allegro
2. Flambée
3. Boheme Bourgeoise
4. V Zátiší
5. Kampa Park

Our top five for atmosphere are:
1. Hergetova Cihelná
2. Kampa Park
3. U Modré Kachnicky
4. Boheme Bourgeoise
5. Le Saint Jacques

Alcron, Štěpánská 40, Nové Město
Tel: 222 820 038 www.radisson.com
Open: 5.30–10.30pm. Closed Sundays.
Seafood   2,000kc

Once rated as the best restaurant in Prague by *Gourmet* (the Czech equivalent to Zagat's restaurant guide) and the winner of the American Academy of Hospitality Sciences' Five Star Diamond Award from 2003 to 2006, Alcron certainly takes its place in the upper echelons of Prague eateries. The buzzwords here are fish, fish and more fish, cooked and prepared with

consummate skill by expert chefs. Although it's a tiny place, located on the ground floor of the Radisson SAS Alcron hotel (see Sleep), with just 24 covers, the venue has an intimacy that transcends its role of hotel restaurant (even if the busy lobby can sometimes intrude on the atmosphere). Based on the same Art Deco theme that extends throughout the hotel, a colourful mural of turn-of-the-century Prague life covers one wall, and an obvious attention to detail – figurative lamps, ornaments, soft lighting – adds to the homely glow of the place. Dishes are often innovative, and deliver a fabulous array of tastes and textures, many of them involving foie gras or black truffles. The wine list includes a comprehensive assortment of New and Old World selections, complete with thorough descriptions and recommendations. A five-course gourmet menu is on offer, with selected wine provided by the glass to complement each dish.

Food 8, Service 8, Atmosphere 7

Allegro, Four Seasons Hotel, Veleslavínova 2, Staré Město

Tel: 221 427 000   www.fourseasons.com
Open: daily, 11.30am–midnight
Mediterranean/Czech   2,000kc

The Allegro offers fine dining at its best. The culinary expertise of this Four Seasons restaurant is beyond question. The Mediterranean/Czech fusion created by chef Vito Mollica (El Bulli and London's Marco Pierre White) is

 superb, the rich flavours and variety of taste sensations truly extraordinary, and the dishes prepared and presented to perfection. The grandiose dining room is conservative – it's not overly stuffy, but it has an air of sterility born of its in-hotel location. The service is immaculate and watchful, and the wine list is extensive (there is no in-house sommelier but the staff are knowledgeable). Although foodies will want to check out Allegro any time of year, summer is by far the best time to come, since guests can dine on the small terrace overlooking the river and the Castle. With a river-level view of the Charles Bridge and Castle lit up spectacularly at night, there could be no better place to feel the magic of Prague than at a table by the window of the Allegro. Reservations are essential.

Food 10, Service 9/10, Atmosphere 8

L'Ardoise, Bruselská 7/ Londinská 29, Vinohrady

Tel: 222 524 102
Open: daily, 11.30am–midnight
French   650kc

Situated in Prague's trendy Vinohrady district, new Prague eaterie L'Ardoise offers sophisticated French food in a wonderfully down-to-earth setting. The

name, French for 'blackboard', is apposite for a spot that chalks its daily specials up in classic Gallic style – and the Francophone touches don't stop there. The menu is resolutely French too, with soups and fish aplenty. The dishes are served in a natural, modern setting that boasts wooden furniture throughout the calm and delightfully unpretentious space. Best of all is the service; both staff and owners add a charming personal touch that doesn't ever stray towards obsequiousness. Additionally, there is an impressive French wine list and a well-informed sommelier, and it is one of the few spots that seems to be genuinely family-friendly. Definitely worth the trip.

Food 8, Service 9/10, Atmosphere 8

Aromi, Mánesova 78, Vinohrady
Tel: 222 713 222   www.aromi.cz
Open: daily, noon–10pm (11pm Fri–Sat)
Italian   750kc

Aromi, another Vinohrady restaurant, has made a more than reputable name for itself in the relatively short amount of time it's been open. Italian through and through, the enchanting space is divided into two distinct areas, both furnished with natural wooden floors and brick walls. The staff are charming, and the menu, which specializes in seafood – Aromi receives fresh catches each day, and around 85% of the menu is fish-based – also offers classic Italian dishes, including a luscious *carpaccio*, lasagne and *risotti*. Meals are simply prepared, but with incredibly fresh ingredients. Aromi's style

leaves each dish heaped with diverse yet complementary flavours. Some of the restaurant's wide varieties of wines are on display, and a large antipasti bar is located in the centre of one of the rooms. Serving consistently good food stylishly and at very reasonable prices, Aromi is one more enjoyable reason to head to Vinohrady.

Food 8, Service 8, Atmosphere 8

Atelier, Na Kovárně 8, Vršovice
Tel: 271 721 866   www.restaurantatelier.cz
Open: noon–midnight. Closed Sundays.
French   600kc

Although Atelier is a long-standing institution in Prague, its future looked uncertain when it lost its head chef and closed down for a short time

during 2006. Happily, when it reopened its reputation as a restaurant to be reckoned with was quickly restored – a necessity, perhaps, given its location a half-hour taxi ride from the centre. Boasting a relaxed but smart interior with modern touches such as skinny-legged tables and plastic cord-backed chairs, Atelier still serves classic French cuisine, including foie gras, fish, lamb and game, and also boasts a flavourful home-made *crème brulée*. Atelier usually offers some interesting daily specials, including the occasional fixed menu and/or business lunch deal (a three-course menu can be pre-arranged for 330kc). In accordance with the name, there are regular art exhibitions. With a fantastic wine list and pleasantly observant service, this is a smart place to spend an afternoon or evening.

Food 8, Service 8/9, Atmosphere 8

Barock, Pařížská 24, Josefov
Tel: 222 329 221
Open: daily, 8.30am (10am Sat–Sun)–1am
Eclectic/Asian   1,500kc

Barock is one of two ultra-glamorous restaurants found on this fashionable shopping street – the other being its sister venue Pravda, just across the road. With a large interior framed with black-and-white fashion prints, floor-

to-ceiling windows, sizeable gilt mirrors and ornate crystal chandeliers, Barock is every bit the celeb hangout. The décor juxtaposes the antique and the contemporary, melding into a French-style brasserie, while the menu, trendily multicultural, has an emphasis  on sushi (with a fine selection of Thai and Japanese dishes too). Barock offers excellent *sake*, and a wine list that draws from cellars around the world. It's certainly chic – some call it pretentious – but there's no denying the quality of the food, nor the inflated prices. Perhaps this simply reflects the price of celeb-spotting in the 21st century.

Food 8, Service 8, Atmosphere 8

Bellevue, Smetanovo nábřeži 18, Staré Město

Tel: 222 221 443   www.bellevuerestaurant.cz
Open: noon–3pm, 5.30–11pm Mon–Sat; 11am–3.30pm, 7–11pm Sun
International   1,500kc

After some fairly extensive renovations, one of the city's more famous high-
end eateries is now open again. Located on the bank of the Old Town side
of the Vltava, Bellevue's obvious appeal remains its location. Nowhere else

can you dine with such a clear
view of Prague Castle and
Charles Bridge, framed by gen-
erously expansive windows. The
newly renovated interior is a
vast improvement. The older,
more formal setting has been
replaced by a slick, contemporary mix of cream tones offset
with purple chairs, carefully
positioned foliage and designer
chandeliers. Along with the
interior renovations, Bellevue
has also revamped its menu.
The selections on offer are
more eclectic these days, and
include fresh fish, traditional
Czech cuisine and innovative
Indian fusions. A piano player provides gentle background music Monday to
Saturday evenings, while on Sunday there is live jazz. There's also a terrace
for summertime dining. It's not one of the cheapest places to eat (entrees
start at around 700kc) but with such great food and views, it's possibly still
good value for money.

Food 8, Service 8, Atmosphere 8

Boheme Bourgeoise, Haštalská 18, Josefov

Tel: 222 311 234 www.ladegustation.cz
Open: 5pm–midnight. Closed Sundays.
International   1,800kc

Brand spanking new and set to create a ripple through Prague's culinary
scene, Boheme Bourgeoise is a must for those who like to combine dégustation, immaculate presentation and cultural history. Sleekly presented, with
black furniture, arched ceilings and funky wall-mounted spotlights that subtly
pick out your food while you relax in a softer backlight, the restaurant

offers three main menus, which change daily according to the availability of
fresh ingredients at the local markets and the whims of the highly skilled
chefs. The traditional menu uses 18th-century recipes from historic regional
cookbooks. The second (continental) menu draws on Italian, British and
French dishes for inspiration. The final menu (international) mixes everything
up in an erudite display of eclectic fusion cooking. You simply sit and wait as
one glorious-tasting dish after another weaves its way to your table, som-
meliers hand-pick the best wines for you, and the chefs busy themselves as
you watch through an opening in the wall. Boheme's service is impeccable,
and while dining here is definitely not cheap, it is highly recommended.

Food 9/10, Service 9/10, Atmosphere 8

Brasserie Ullmann, Letenské Sady 341, P7

Tel: 233 378 200   www.letenskyzamecek.cz
Open: daily, 11am–11pm
Czech/French   450kc

A small designer brasserie, Ullmann is set in Letenské Sady – a park stretching down from the Castle to the river on the north side of the city. Upstairs is an exceptionally smart, reservations-only restaurant, while in the garden there is a simpler terrace space, where you can enjoy beer in plastic cups among topless teenagers. Inside, Brasserie Ullmann is simple and modern, retaining some of the Art Deco characteristics that the city so casually exudes, and a fair amount of glass means that the lines are fresh and

uncomplicated. The menu is seasonal and the specials change at different times of the year to incorporate truffles, oysters and seasonal game. The menu includes an interesting combination of Czech and French dishes, making good use of local goose and rabbit. The staff are proactive and friendly, and Ullmann is a great place to come to after a head-clearing Saturday morning walk, combining spectacular views of the Old Town stretched out below with good-quality food and service.

Food 7/8, Service 8, Atmosphere 7

Le Café Colonial, Široká 6, Josefov
Tel: 224 818 322
Open: daily, 10am–midnight
French/International   900kc

This colourful, funky café-restaurant deep in the heart of the Jewish Quarter, with its walls painted in deep reds, blues, yellows and greens, is hugely popular with local Josefovs and tourists alike. The café section (to the right as you enter the main door) is comfortable and suitable for a casual

lunch and a cosy chat. The main restaurant is slightly more overwhelming, with huge wrought-iron, Art Deco chandeliers hanging from the ceiling, a giant love-heart mural on the far wall and designer tables and chairs vying for your attention. The stylish menu heralds a high standard of cuisine drawn from a predominantly French menu, but tinged with Italian and international selections and the occasional regional flourish. The wine list is complete, with a small choice of Czech and some reasonably priced Italian and French dishes. All in all, a tasteful but relaxed dining option and very good value for money.

Food 7/8, Service 7/8, Atmosphere 8

Cowboys, Nerudova 40, Malá Strana
Tel 296 826 107 www.kampagroup.com
Open: daily, noon–11pm
Steak   800kc

Having already revamped one of Prague's more famous restaurants (Bazaar), the Kampa Group have now created in its place a brand new, and very themed, steak house. Of course, this is a steak house with panache and style, complete with denim-wearing staff, cowhide banquettes, a funky bar (with sports screens), DJs on weekends and a summer terrace that offers truly formidable views – well, aside from the tacky plastic rotating cow that seems to be on permanent display. More importantly, the high-end steaks (beef, pork, lamb and veal) that the restaurant serves have justifiably become the talk of the town. There's also a range of other highlights on the menu: chicken wings, Italian salads, fish and seafood dishes and a variety of sides to

complement your meal. Plenty of Pilsner Urquell, Miller and fine wines are also on hand to help you wash it all down. More moderately priced than many Kampa Park spots, Cowboys makes for a fun night out.

Food 8, Service 8, Atmosphere 8

David, Tržiště 21, Malá Strana
Tel: 257 533 109   www.restaurant-david.cz
Open: daily, 11.30am–11pm
Czech/French   900kc

Nestled away in the labyrinthine back streets beneath the Castle, David is something of a gourmet's paradise, offering delicately prepared dishes served by charming and friendly staff. It's independently run, and small (40 covers), and the maître d' and chef owners are often on hand to ensure that

everything proceeds smoothly. Décor-wise David is a little on the conservative side – all antique furniture and original paintings – but the affable ambience tends to thaw any starchiness pretty quickly. The Czech/French menu isn't hugely extensive

but is very particular, crammed with freshly prepared, intricate dishes and subtle combinations. If you're lucky enough to dine here on a warm evening, you can take advantage of the small outdoor terrace.

Food 8, Service 9, Atmosphere 7

Essensia, Mandarin Oriental Hotel, Nebovidska 1, Malá Strana

Tel: 233 088 777   www.mandarinoriental.com
Open: noon–2.30pm, 7–10.30pm Mon–Sat; 7–10pm Sun
Asian/Modern European   1,000kc

Despite its location inside the Mandarin Oriental hotel, Essensia is far from being stuffy or conservative. Comprising five adjoining rooms crowned by vaulted ceilings, the main rooms offer a soft-hued elegance and an urbanity that is reflected in its subtly refined food. A combination of Asian and modern European cuisine enlivens the menu, executed with authenticity rather

than with the prevalent ethos of trendy fusion cooking. The dishes, immaculately presented, are highly memorable, suffused with fresh ingredients and wonderful sauces. There is an extensive wine list that offers vintages from France, Italy and the New World, as well as an exclusive selection from the best regional wineries. Service is as punctilious as you'd expect from a five-star environment, although it's also nicely informal. A wonderful dining experience in a high-end setting.

Food 9, Service 9, Atmosphere 8

Flambée, Husova 5, Staré Město

Tel: 224 248 512   www.flambee.cz
Open: daily, 11.30am–1am
Czech/French   2,000kc

One of Prague's more elegant and accomplished restaurants, this converted 8th-century cellar opened in 1993 and immediately won international awards for its design. Refurbished after the 2002 floods, the space has retained its air of semi-formal yet fairly romantic elegance, helped along notably by a loyal clientele who tend to be slightly older and grander than

elsewhere. The menu offers a decidedly gourmet experience – beautifully prepared dishes cooked to perfection – and includes a special five-course set menu selected by the chef, as well as plenty of truffle combinations (if you're lucky enough to be there in the right season). Backing up Flambée's food is a superlative wine list that includes an inordinate number of top French selections and an in-house sommelier to guide you through the multiple choices; there's also a pianist most evenings, and the opportunity to dine among the rich and famous.

Food 9, Service 9, Atmosphere 8/9

Francouzská, Obecní Dům, nám Republiky 5, Staré Město

Tel: 222 002 770   www.obecnidum.cz
Open: daily, noon–4pm, 6–11pm
Czech/International   1,450kc

Perhaps the most distinguished of all the restaurants in Prague, Francouszká is located within the Municipal House, one of the city's most impressive Art Nouveau buildings. Sharing the same architectural character as its host edifice, the dining room of Francouszká is a large, open room with stunning gold chandeliers, cylindrical glass and wall

lights, all topped with an awe-inspiring 30-foot painted ceiling. Settle into a dark green leather banquette behind an expanse of pristine white tablecloth covered in fine Bohemian crystal, and drift back a century or so as you browse the menu. An erudite blend of traditional Czech and world cuisine, the food is generally top-notch (specialities include lobster bisque and *coq au vin*). In the same building are an equally impressive Kavarna (see Snack) and beautiful concert hall. The restaurant runs packages, including tickets to a concert and a set three-course menu for 1,700kc – good value for a night of sophisticated food and classical entertainment.

Food 8, Service 8/9, Atmosphere 8

Hergetova Cihelná, Cihelná 2b, Malá Strana
Tel. 257 535 534   www.cihelna.com
Open: daily, 9am–2am
Eclectic   900kc

A younger sibling of the legendary Kampa Park, the fun-to-pronounce Hergetova Cihelná has managed to impress on its own terms. While it shares Kampa Park's stunning views of Charles Bridge and the Old Town, its menu and concept differ. Set up as a bar/lounge and restaurant, the emphasis has been subtly shifted from dining to socializing, although there's certainly no shirking on the quality, presentation or flavour of the food. The restaurant itself is spread over two floors. Upstairs is a separate pizzeria; downstairs there's a long bar, main dining room and gorgeous terrace, which comes alive in the summer when DJs turn up and weave designer soundtracks. The building itself dates from the 18th century and used to be a

brick factory (*cihelná*), but is now decorated with modern yet comfortable furnishings by top Czech designer Barbora Skorpilová. The menu is, inevitably, an eclectic combination of tastes, merging the flavours of the Far East with those of Italy and Central Europe. Like Kampa Park, Cihelná draws a sophisticated crowd of movers and shakers, although dining here tends to be a surprisingly relaxed and unpretentious experience.

Food 8, Service 8/9, Atmosphere 9

Hot, Václavské náměstí 45, Nové Město
Tel: 222 247 240   www.hotrestaurant.cz
Open: daily, 6.30am–1am
Eclectic   1,000kc

Until recently, Wenceslas Square was largely the antithesis of culinary cool: an unpretentious shopping area, with the occasional hotel and peppering of drinking holes. The designer steamroller has arrived, however, and the square now looks set to become increasingly trendy. Hot is one of the first such establishments in the vicinity. Owned by Bacchus, the people behind Pravda and Barock, the restaurant brings some much-needed style to the area in the form of a catch-all café-bar-restaurant that is both highly chic and highly priced. It's a fairly vivid place, where new Prague meets old; modern décor (glass, metal and wood materials, Capellini lights and a white, red and black theme) nestle within a turn-of-the-century building complete with Art Deco accents and a wonderful staircase. Offering 130 types of wine from around the world, DJs, themed nights, live music, celebrities and piano players, Hot can provide a seriously good night out (watch out for the go-go

dancers every Saturday), as well as an innovative dining experience. The kitchen fuses East with West and is well known for creating decent sushi and Thai dishes. Veggie options are available, and while the lighter lunch menu (sandwiches and salads heavy) is good for those on the go, the dinner selections are as eclectic as the surroundings.

Food 8, Service 8, Atmosphere 8

Kampa Park, Na Kampá 8b, Malá Strana
Tel: 257 532 685/6 www.kampapark.com
Open: daily, 11.30am–1am
International   1,400kc

The don dada of Prague's gourmet scene, Kampa Park opened in the early

1990s, and has consistently ranked among the city's restaurant elite ever since. Founded by Swedish impresario Nils Jebens, it has become the flagship of a culinary empire that includes Square and Cihelná, as well as recent acquisitions La Provence (page 97) and Cowboys (page 79). Fêted for its high standards, Kampa's menu is a real treat – not only does it draw from the Czech Republic's natural pantry, but it has also succeeded in creating an almost seamless amalgamation of cuisines from around the world. Like the food, the design of the restaurant is modern and stylish. Kampa is split into three sections: the main restaurant is restrained and sophisticated, the smaller dining room overlooking the river is quiet and elegant, while the water-level terrace is light, airy and relaxing. Kampa Park is definitely worth a visit, but since it's a Prague institution that retains its popularity year round, ensure that you book ahead.

Food 9, Service 8/9, Atmosphere 9

Khajuraho, Michalská 19, Staré Město
Tel: 225 77 73 33   www.khajuraho.cz
Open: daily, 11am–11pm
Indian   1,200kc

Prague doesn't exactly have a wide range of curry houses, so the appear-

ance of this brand new dedicated Indian restaurant, located in the cellar of the Iron Gate Hotel (see Sleep) is more than welcome. Khajuraho's aim is to provide high-end Indian cuisine for a five-star clientele, offering not only classic North Indian dishes but also regional southern dishes, such as masala dosas. The décor is fairly formal – imported fabrics and furnishings create an authentic Indian ambience – but the prices are definitely more Prague than Kerala. The kitchen is capable of turning out some tremendous food (without a doubt the best of its kind in town), but on quiet nights the chefs seem to relax too much and food can be, like the service, mediocre. If you're craving Indian cuisine, this is the place to come, but try to make it here at the weekend, when the seats are full and you'll perhaps have a chance to catch some classical Indian music and dance accompaniments.

Food 8, Service 7, Atmosphere 7

Kogo, Na Příkopě 22, Nové Město
Tel: 221 451 259 www.kogo.cz
Open: daily, 11am–11pm
Italian   800kc

The second restaurant in the ever-expanding Kogo chain has proved to be as successful as the original entity. Situated in the atrium of the Slovansky Dum shopping centre on Na Příkopě, this sharp but affable Italian eaterie has become a popular haunt for politicians, media execs and successful ex-pats. You can sit outside on the expansive terrace or pull up a chair in the smart, crisp interior. It's distinctly upmarket by most shopping-centre

standards, and its constantly buzzing atmosphere, quick and efficient service and consistently good food (at realistic prices) means that Kogo is always in vogue. Ideal for a relaxing evening meal, a snappy business lunch or even a quick bite pre- or post-theatre.

Food 8, Service 8, Atmosphere 8

Kolkovna, V Kolkovně 8, Josefov

Tel. 224 819 701 www.kolkovna.cz
Open: daily, 11am–midnight
Czech   400kc

Kolkovna is a modern Czech beer hall decorated in Art Nouveau style. It's not only the décor that conjures up an old-school feel, however. The knowing, vaguely efficient waiters, Pilsner Urquell on draught (it's owned by the

brewery) and a menu that offers such traditional Czech classics as Moravian sparrow, pork knuckle and Pilsen Goulash, all add to the traditional allure of this place. The menu is far broader than you might expect from a local spot, and attempts to include modern and international cuisine – innovative hors d'ouevres appear alongside the 'Things To Eat With Beer' menu, for example. A slightly more breezy and refreshing establishment than many traditional spots, and in a very good location (central, but away from the main tourist draws), Kolkovna provides comfortable meals in a somewhat nostalgic environment.

Food 6, Service 7, Atmosphere 7

Lary Fary, Dlouhá 30, Josefov

Tel: 222 320 154 www.laryfary.cz
Open: daily, 11am–midnight
Eclectic   1,000kc

Set in a baroque building halfway down Dlouhá, Lary Fary is part of a new breed of restaurants trying to appeal to all and sundry. Serving up a waywardly eclectic range of food – from Brazilian-style churascos to Greek mezze, Japanese sushi and Italian pastas – the menu is truly international.

Gigantic skewers (meat, fish, vegetables) that dangle tantalizingly from hooks suspended over your table are the house specialty, and prove a memorable experience. The venue itself is intimate and discreet: a small street-level spot with vaulted ceilings in the main dining areas and an underground feel. The attentive and tactful staff seem to know their stuff, and the restaurant is careful to set couples apart from larger parties to offer a little more intimacy. A variety of live music can be enjoyed some nights of the week, and this can provide welcome distraction when culinary standards occasionally slip (dishes can taste bland or even a little cold). Come here if you want a wide choice, but be aware that the prices are ridiculously inflated.

Food 7/8, Service 8, Atmosphere 8

Lehka Hlava, Boršov 2, Staré Město
Tel: 222 220 665   www.lehkahlava.cz
Open: 11.30am–midnight Mon–Fri; noon–11.30pm Sat–Sun
Vegetarian   350kc

Vegetarian restaurants don't get much funkier than this. To be found along a side street off Karoliny Světlé (close to Duende, see Drink), Lehka Hlava ('Clear Head') impresses in several ways. From the open kitchen, where you can see the chefs cheerfully work away behind a bar-like area while a member of staff seats you, to the fantastic décor, this restaurant makes an impact. With a coruscating wonderland of detail (ceilings filled with glittering

stars, curvaceous fireplaces, fish tanks, projections and colourful, striped walls), the interior offers pleasing distractions aplenty. The restaurant also has a private salon and even a tiny courtyard, resplendent in bamboo. The menu, wholly vegetarian, is also impressive. An appealingly healthy range of pastas, salads, couscous, *bulgar*, *quesadillas* and vegetables defies those who claim that vegetarian food is boring and undistinguished. True, Lehka Hlava doesn't serve haute cuisine, but everything is far tastier than dedicated carnivores might suppose. Continuing the healthy bent, a range of non-alcoholic beverages is available, including special teas, fresh juices and a delectable Aztec chocolate with chilli and walnut, although there are wines aplenty to choose from, and specials each day. Refreshingly, it's non-smoking.

Food 7/8, Service 8, Atmosphere 9

Mlynec, Novotného lávka 9, Staré Město
Tel: 221 082 208   www.group.cz
Open: daily, noon–3pm, 5.30–11pm
Czech/International   1,300kc

Sandwiched between two of Prague's most popular tourist clubs, and just a disco beat from Charles Bridge, Mlynec is more upmarket than you might imagine from its nondescript exterior. Having been washed away in the floods of 2002, the restaurant (part of the highly regarded V Zátiší catering group) is kitted out with green carpets patterned with gold fleurs-de-lis, antiquated curtains and tapestries, and a heavily spotlighted ceiling. If it all sounds depressingly formal, don't worry: the food – wonderful combinations

of traditional Czech and refreshing Far Eastern dishes – is famously good, and the views of the river, bridge and Castle are peerless. Popular with business people and wealthy locals, Mlynec also offers a surprisingly romantic option for discerning visitors.

Food 8, Service 9, Atmosphere 7

U Modré Kachničky 2, Michalská 16, Staré Město
Tel: 224 213 418   www.umodrekachnicky.cz
Open: daily, 11.30am–11.30pm
Czech   700kc

The second version of this Prague dining institution is conveniently located in the Old Town, not far from Old Town Square. Famous for its hearty, quintessentially Czech cuisine, it specializes in game and duck dishes (the name

translates as 'The Blue Duck'), but offers other options including steaks, fish and also vegetarian dishes. Occupying two floors, both quaintly embellished by 1930s and '40s swing and jazz, it's an undeniably romantic place. The downstairs is darker and more intimate, while upstairs can be used to cater for larger parties and groups. The wine list features a decent range of Czech and French varieties and the waiters are knowledgeable enough to help you choose the best wine for your meal. The food is good – very good – but don't be surprised to find you feel somewhat heavier on leaving than when you first went in.

Food 8, Service 9, Atmosphere 8

Mozaika, Nitranská 13, Vinohrady
Tel: 224 253 011 www.restaurantmozaika.cz
Open: daily, 11.30am–midnight
Czech   400kc

Rapidly gentrifying Vinohrady is becoming home to Prague's middle classes. The relative increase in wealth has seen the opening of new bars, restaurants and clubs aimed at young, upwardly mobile Czechs, as opposed to just tourists. Mozaika is definitely one of the more atmospheric and inexpensive restaurants springing up to meet new local demands. Just a short taxi ride from the Old Town, the restaurant has had the critics and budget hedonists

(as well as locals) raving. The long, light yellow cellar space fills up quickly on weekend evenings, so make a reservation. While the décor is nothing special, the food most certainly is – especially at prices that are well below Old

Town standard. The daily menu, chalked up on a blackboard over the bar, is supplemented by excellent permanent dishes that include orientally inspired and infused concoctions, as well as Prague's most widely acclaimed burgers. Add the informal service and the tingling sensation of being far from the trodden tourist paths, and you have an all-round triumph on your hands.

Food 7/8, Service 7/8, Atmosphere 8

Nostress Café, Dušní 10, Josefov

Tel. 222 317 007   www.nostress.cz
Open: daily, 8am (10am Sat–Sun)–11pm
Asian/French   650kc

French–Asian café-restaurant Nostress recently underwent a refurbishment that has pointed the establishment towards the higher end of Prague's dining hierarchy. Its central location (just a short stroll from Old Town Square, over the road from Kolkovna) is still a major draw, but the elegant and sophisticated ambience and interesting, tasty menu seal the deal. The linear and funky décor is much more avant-Asian than fusty French, with deep reds, auburns and blacks colluding lasciviously. More contemporary touches,

including an abundance of foliage and red lamps that hang like giant chillies in front of pleasingly large windows, add a gentle ambience. A smaller café/bar area serves sandwiches and light meals, while the main room menu – casual and lounge-esque in the daytime, sumptuous in the evening – boasts all manner of interesting and exotic East–West fusions. Furniture fans may want to slink downstairs to the basement, where they will find a ware-

93

house full of the imported furnishings and curios that inhabit the main restaurant.

Food 7, Service 8, Atmosphere 8

Palffy Palac, Valdštejnská 14, Malá Strana
Tel: 257 530 522
Open: daily, 11am–midnight
Czech   1,000kc

Slightly off the main tourist route, to one side of Malostranské Náměstí, this classic restaurant is situated in a palace that dates back to the Lamintger family of the 17th century. To get to the food, follow your nose and climb the large baroque staircase (bathed in candlelight at night) past the music schools and up to the top floor. The main dining room, dark and romantic, is immediately impressive. A beautiful, gilded chandelier hangs from the high ceiling, and every table is slightly different, giving the impression that a dining experience here is unique and special. On the walls are  portraits and photographs of Prague in its halcyon days, and the menu boasts a similarly nostalgic range of traditional Czech food, such as wild duck *carpaccio* and roast quail. There's a smaller room for diners requiring a little more intimacy, and in the summer months the large terrace is opened, affording fantastic views over the rooftops towards the Old Town. Whether you're looking for a romantic meal or simply a quiet, memorable experience, Palffy Palac will fulfil all your needs.

Food 8, Service 8, Atmosphere 8

Parnas, Smetanovo Nábřeži 2, Staré Město
Tel: 224 218 493   www.restaurantparnas.cz
Open: daily, 6pm–midnight
Czech   900kc

The sister restaurant to the famous Café Slavia next door (see Snack),
Parnas is situated in a similarly magnificent Art Deco room with wonderfully
ornate wood-panelled walls, stone floors and superb views across the river
and up towards the Castle. The Czech menu concentrates on meat and
game, with the rabbit and *goulash* particularly hard to beat for taste. The

Czech wine list complements the food, but some more established tipples
are on offer for those a little unsure of the local viniculture. A pianist in the
corner helps personalize the atmosphere, making it worth the trip just to
experience the wonderful evening ambience. It's just a stone's throw from
the National Theatre, too, so consider this for a pre- or post-opera dinner.

Food 8, Service 8, Atmosphere 8

U Patrona, Dražického Náměstí 4, Malá Strana
Tel: 257 530 725
Open: daily, 11am–midnight
French   1,000kc

A small restaurant set in a townhouse just to the north of Charles Bridge,
U Patrona features a light, spacious and elegantly furnished dining room
downstairs, and a smaller, more sophisticated upstairs space (even with an

intimate balcony for two). One of the added pleasures of eating up here is the windowed view into the kitchen, where you can watch the chefs busying themselves with your meal. The French menu highlights the easy fusion between traditional Gallic cooking and the Czech Republic's natural larder, with the inevitable emphasis on meat and indigenous game. The decidedly lovely, old-fashioned atmosphere can occasionally be marred by the ubiquitous tourist groups keen to take advantage of U Patrona's good location and nostalgic style. If it's intimacy you seek, make sure there are no group bookings when you make a reservation.

Food 8, Service 9, Atmosphere 8

La Perle de Prague, Rašínovo nábřeži 80, Nové Město
Tel: 221 984 160 www.laperle.cz
Open: noon–2pm, 7–10.30pm. Closed Sunday and Monday lunch.
French   1,300kc

Set at the top of Frank Gehry's controversial 'Fred & Ginger' building (Prague's most talked-about example of modern architecture), this restaurant in 'the Pearl of Prague' offers breathtaking views that take in Castle and everything else all the way to Vyšehrad. Finding it can be the most difficult part of your evening, as the entrance is not immediately apparent, hidden inside a small, often quiet café to one side; from here you are shown up to the seventh floor. Split over two levels, the upstairs offers access to the terrace with a few tables for pre- or post-dinner drinks and romantic rooftop moments, while downstairs a formal, more elegant and modern interior sets the tone for your dining indulgences. The clientele tend to be well-heeled

and smartly dressed – upmarket locals, international business people and a few, romantically inclined holiday-makers – and the menu is primarily French, offering a broad selection of game, meat, fish and seafood, washed down with an extensive selection of French wine. Service is impeccable and a meal here more than memorable.

Food 8, Service 9, Atmosphere 9

Pravda, Pařížská 17, Josefov

Tel: 222 326 303   www.pravdarestaurant.cz
Open: 8.30am–2am Mon–Fri; 10am–2am Sat; 10am–1am Sun
International   1,200kc

A decidedly glamorous restaurant on the fashionable shopping street Pařížská, Pravda ('truth') is located opposite its sister restaurant, Barock

(see page 75). It's designed and decorated in the classic French brasserie style, with pristine white tablecloths, a long, elegant bar and mirrors that increase the feeling of space. The food is, surprisingly enough, much more international, with a mixture of European and Asian cuisine working to create interesting fusions. More than capable of luring the odd celebrity within its doors, Pravda offers an al-fresco option in summer that provides equally interesting people-watching opportunities on the streets outside. And although lunch can sometimes be interrupted by passing tour groups, the evening offers greater menu choices and a more intimate atmosphere. There's a good wine list and a cocktail menu to ensure you can enjoy yourself late into the night. If the high prices don't quite seem to add up at the end, that's probably because you didn't include the additional cost of cool.

Food 7/8, Service 8, Atmosphere 8

La Provence, Štupartská 9, Staré Město
Tel: 296 826 155 www.laprovence.cz
Open: daily, 11am–11pm
French/Mediterranean   1,000kc

One of Prague's more established restaurants, La Provence was recently amalgamated into the ever-expanding Kampa Park chain. The atmosphere of the cosy, intimate downstairs, with its floral cushions and eclectic furnishings, remains its lovable old self, and even the same classic Provence menu is on offer. Upstairs is a somewhat smarter Art Deco/Art Nouveau brasserie, with large windows overlooking the streets behind Tyn Church. The upstairs contrasts neatly with the darkened, intimate atmosphere downstairs, making

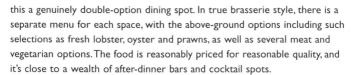

this a genuinely double-option dining spot. In true brasserie style, there is a separate menu for each space, with the above-ground options including such selections as fresh lobster, oyster and prawns, as well as several meat and vegetarian options. The food is reasonably priced for reasonable quality, and it's close to a wealth of after-dinner bars and cocktail spots.

Food 7, Service 8, Atmosphere 8

Rybí Trh, Týn 5, Staré Město
Tel: 224 895 447   www.flambee.cz
Open: daily, 11am–midnight
Seafood   1,100kc

Tucked away behind Old Town Square in a quiet courtyard full of little bars and restaurants, Rybí Trh is famous for its delicious fish. In the summer the restaurant has a charming outdoor terrace – a perfect suntrap for balmy lunches alongside fashionistas hiding behind designer sunglasses. The choice consists almost entirely of seafood and fish, with a couple of token meat

dishes and vegetable side dishes thrown in for good measure. You can choose your selections from the ice drift or straight from the fish tanks that surround the simply decorated interior. A wide-ranging wine list includes an interesting selection of Old and New World wines, all taken from the wine shop next door, and available to purchase for a picnic in the park. All in all, this location is an astute choice for seafood lovers, while the wine shop itself is well worth a quick trip if you are interested in stocking up on some fine Moravian wines before you return home.

Food 9, Service 8, Atmosphere 8

Sahara Café, Ibsenova 1, Vinohrady

Tel: 222 514 987
Open: daily, 8am–midnight
Eclectic   700kc

A striking new café on the corner of Náměstí Míru, Sahara is run by an
Italian brother and sister team, who have worked hard to create their
dream project. The space reflects their attention to detail, and is immediate-

ly impressive. Tall windows and
calm, sandy colours draw you in
off the street and once inside
you're enveloped by a wealth of
exotic elements, from Buddhist
statues and masks to perfect
Asian seating areas and vigorous
palms. The main café gives way to
a seemingly endless labyrinth of
similarly immaculate spaces suitable for lunches or dinners,
including a quiet garden area in
summertime. The dinner menu
offers a vague selection of Indian
tandoori and Middle Eastern

dishes, alongside Italo-Mediterranean fare. A wood oven heats up a number
of entrées, and a meticulously selected wine collection can definitely keep
up with the heat. While not perfect, the food here is above-average and is
bound to improve over time. Prices for meals can get expensive, but so
charming is the space and so pleasant the service that you probably won't
mind.

Food 7/8, Service 8/9, Atmosphere 9

Le Saint Jacques, Jakubovská 4, Staré Město

Tel: 222 322 685 www.saint-jacques.cz
Open: noon–3pm, 6pm–midnight. Closed Sat and Sun lunch.
French   1,000kc

A small, backstreet French bistro, lodged between some of Prague's livelier
student bars, St Jacques is one of the more fun places to eat in the city. The

food is good, but the real reason to come here is its pair of musicians – a pianist and violinist who are found in the restaurant every night talking, joking and taking requests from the diners. Even if it's a quiet night they'll liven it up with tunes ranging from Cole Porter and Elvis to haunting gypsy ballads. Towards the end of the evening, once sufficient alcohol has been imbibed, diners are coaxed onto their feet to dance between the tables by flickering candlelight. The classic French menu is filled with customary dishes: frogs' legs, snails and an excellent *Coquilles Saint-Jacques* are available, all complemented by a selection of French regional wines. With food choices that can range in quality between courses but always delight in portion, this is definitely one for the incurable romantics.

Food 7, Service 8, Atmosphere 9

La Scène, U Milosrdných 6, Josefov
Tel: 222 312 677 www.lascene.cz
Open: daily, 7pm–midnight
French   1,250kc

La Scène is all things to all men: a gourmet restaurant, design masterpiece (complete with a champagne and cigar bar as well as a café), and, ultimately, a place to see and be seen. Chef Rob André Toet creates innovative Francophile dishes, which look as good as the restaurant's swanky interior. The space is separated into sub-sections via subtly raised platforms and coloured fabrics of autumnal yellows and rustic reds, with the central area usually reserved for groups and the smaller side areas more suited to couples and intimate parties. Alongside the memorable food – the menu is small

but refined – is an excellent wine list. You can take an aperitif in the funky lounge on the way in, and clamber downstairs after your meal to the swish Champagne Club if you so desire. Service can be nonchalant at times, but in general it's in keeping with the slick professionalism of the place. If you fancy a more lively ambience, try making an appearance at the weekend, when there are often DJs or live jazz/Latin bands.

Food 8, Service 7, Atmosphere 7

Soho +, Podolské Nábřeží 1, Podoli
Tel: 244 463 772/ 244 462 083   www.sohorestaurant.cz
Open: daily, 11.20am–midnight
Eclectic   600kc

Soho is a stylish new spot, just out of town and set on the Vltava.
Combining the funkiness of a clubbers' lounge with a decent kitchen, this

space has become popular with local fashionistas and young-minded business folk alike, who are willing to ignore the slightly out-of-the-way location to dine somewhere slightly different. Drapes separate the areas within the restaurant, which consist of a main eating space and a chill-out section with comfy sofas. The large windows create a feeling of space and light, and also offer views of the lesser known, but pleasant, views of Vltava's rocky shores. The menu is surprisingly broad, touching on French, Greek, Italian and Japanese food. With selections encompassing *bruschetta*, *carpaccios*, *borscht*, *bouillabaisse*, *sushi* and *risotti*, pasta and grilled meats, the restaurant caters for most tastes. Just when you thought the place couldn't get any cooler, Soho also serves Stella on tap.

Food 7/8, Service 8, Atmosphere 8

La Veranda, Eliška Krásnohorské 2, Josefov
Tel: 224 814 733 www.laveranda.cz
Open: daily, 11am (4pm Sun)–11pm
Asian Fusion   900kc

Located in trendy Josefov, La Veranda is the epitome of a contemporary restaurant in a fashionable area. The basic layout relies on a contrast of colours, combined with architecturally clean lines, resulting in an intimate, smart aura.

Although it is located below street level, large windows throw generous amounts of light into the room. The menu is based on an East-meets-West fusion, and is deliciously devoid of fats and fatty meats, preferring innovation and freshness to substantial, filling cuisine. A selection of different menus (including a dégustation menu) is designed to reflect award-winning chef Radek David's interest in different taste combinations and sensations. This café can offer a refreshing, healthier change from the heavier meals to be found around the city.

Food 8, Service 8, Atmosphere 8

Yami, Masná 3, Staré Město
Tel: 222 312 756 www.sushi-yami.cz
Open: daily, 11am–11.30pm
Japanese/Korean   700kc

Sushi seems to be the latest culinary craze in Prague, with a spate of restaurants opening across the city in the past few years. Many of these offer average fare and are set inside sterile shopping centres. Yami, a Japanese and Korean restaurant, successfully manages to combine a down-to-earth yet intimate atmosphere with authentic cuisine. Just a short walk from Old

Town Square (and dangerously close to the Triangle of Sin), the interior is immediately appealing, with its simple orange and black décor, abundance of foliage and beaming chefs. Both the Korean and sushi menus tick all the expected boxes: *wakame* and *miso* soup, *nigiri*, *maki* and hand-rolled sushi are on offer, as well as Korean specialties that include grilled pork with vegetables, seaweed omelettes with spring onion and spicy fish soup, and most importantly, kim-chee with decent amounts of chilli. While prices are fairly high, they're no higher than the other sushi joints in town and the selections here are fresh and flavourful.

Food 7/8, Service 8, Atmosphere 7

Zahrada v Opeře, Legerova 75, Nové Město

Tel: 224 239 685   www.zahradavopere.cz
Open: daily, 11.30am–1am
Asian Fusion   1,100kc

Another definitive favourite, and part of a great night out when combined with a trip to the state opera, the Zahrada v Opeře ('Garden of the Opera') is a stunning place to dine. With a zen-like interior created by Bára Skorpilová, one of the city's best young designers, this locale offers a slick, contemporary but natural feel. The wooden floors, slatted walls and

wrought-iron partitions are skilfully balanced with a variety of artifacts that include plants, stone and glass. The menu is as eclectic as the design: part European, part Asian, with a particular emphasis on fish. The food may not be devastatingly original, but there is a good selection of delicious dishes, all beautifully presented.

Food 8, Service 8, Atmosphere 8

V Zátiší, Liliová 1, Staré Město

Tel: 222 221 155   www.pfd.cz
Open: daily, noon–3pm, 5.30–11pm
Eclectic   1,700kc

V Zátiší is the third restaurant in the trilogy (with Bellevue and Mlynec), and is regarded as one of the best restaurants in the country. As with the other members of this chain, the emphasis is on creating a grand overall dining experience. Aimed at a decidedly upmarket clientele, the exquisite food is paired with just as outstanding formal service. A flamboyant 2006 refurbishment has successfully done away with the restaurant's former stiffness, but the reason to come here remains very much the food. The menu offers an eclectic mix of international and domestic fare, drawing ingredients from across the world to  create an array of superb dishes. Ever-changing dégustation menus are available alongside the à la carte choices and, although this is one of the most expensive places to dine in Prague (keep in mind this means that it is around the same price as an average London meal), V Zátiší consistently provides one of the best experiences. Make a reservation, dress up, and look forward to a venture that allows you to experience the culinary talents of chef Jacques Affrays while admiring the artistic eye candy.

Food 9, Service 9, Atmosphere 8

U Zlaté Studně, U Zlaté Studně 4, Malá Strana
Tel: 257 533 322 www.zlatastudna.cz
Open: daily, 7am–11pm
French   800kc

Part of the hotel of the same name, The Golden Well offers outstanding views, a wide selection of wines and enjoyable food. The restaurant is spread over two levels, with the downstairs decorated in a simple but modern style featuring contemporary furnishings and crisp, white tablecloths. The large windows offer a fabulous panorama of Prague, while the upstairs boasts a beautiful open terrace, which is fantastic for summer evenings, winter lunches, and drinks overlooking the city. The menu is international with a leaning towards French cuisine, producing a delicious selection of fish, meat and

game. With an above-average wine list on offer, light jazz piped into the atmosphere and a relaxing and chilled environment, this is one well worth falling into.

Food 8, Service 8, Atmosphere 8

drink...

The consumption of alcohol is virtually a national pastime in the Czech Republic. Since the Czechs were the original producers of Pilsner and Budvar (Budweiser) – along with many other fine lagers with unpronounceable names – it will come as no surprise that pubs and bars here are an integral part of local life.

Pubs, traditionally and predominantly the domain of Czech men, are often simple affairs, rough around the edges and serving little more than a perfect pint of the local beer (but if you're in luck you might get some fried cheese and dumplings). Sometimes unwelcoming or slightly intimidating for women, Czech pubs generally refuse to change their traditional ways and are pretty much a law unto themselves; think of them, perhaps, as a kind of cultural institution.

Bars have come a long way in Prague owing to the influx of tourists over the last decade. Cosy, low-lit cellar bars are the order of the day, while recent years have borne witness to a surge of glossy cocktail and wine bars, located mainly (but not exclusively) to the north of Old Town Square in the so-called 'Triangle of Sin'.

Late-night haunts such as Tretters, the Alcohol Bar and Bombay tend to be populated by party-hearty Czechs and tourists, happy to pay the exorbitant drinks prices in order to get down to bad pop music, and pout, pose and prowl to their heart's content.

SoNa, to the south of the National Theatre, is home to a slightly more alternative crowd. Less chintzy and pretentious than the Old Town, the drinking spots down this way are more authentic and convivial. At places such as the Globe and Ultramarin you can find cheaper drinks, a cooler clientele and an emphasis on chatting and hanging out rather than on pulling and posing. Another attraction of the area is that it does not seem to hold much allure for stag parties.

A third, if low-key, contender is Malá Strana, the district at the foot of the Castle on the west bank of the Vltava. Here the bars attract tourists who are either staying in the area or popping in for a quiet, early evening drink. Particularly recommended are the mellow jazz-cellar Blue Light and the relaxed St Nicholas' Café.

Cafés can play just as important a role in Prague's nocturnal scene as bars. Such places as Café Café are open late into the night, populated by sophisticates who like to while away the evening with wine or herbal tea. Some restaurants also have bars worth hanging in, pre- or post-dinner: Hergetova Cihelná and Square (see Eat) are two fine examples.

Many bars (especially in the centre) are busy on weeknights but, as with any city, weekends throw up the best parties. Few bars have door policies and unless it's a live music venue or nightclub, chances are you won't be paying to get in. Some establishments actively discourage or prohibit large groups of men from entering, which means marauding stag parties are kept at bay, particularly in the smarter spots.

Despite rising prices, drinks remain cheap by British or even European standards: in a local pub a half-litre of beer should cost about 40kc (£1) while in the bigger bars in town you can expect to pay about 60-70kc (£1.50), or even more if you're a tourist in a bar on Old Town Square.

It's worth trying some of the local wines, but it also pays to be picky. Many Czech/Moravian wine lists hide some nasty surprises as well as some nice ones, so try to get a shop recommendation, do some research on the best local wines before you go, or, even better, try a few different recommended choices by the glass in various restaurants or wine bars. Cocktails are normally sold at around 120kc (£3), although prices vary according to the strength of the drink and the salubriousness of the location.

Alcohol Bar, Dušní 6, Josefov

Tel: 224 811 744 www.alcoholbar.cz
Open: daily, 7pm–2am

Situated just behind Old Town Square, rubbing suggestively against the hem of Josefov, the Alcohol Bar wins no awards for titular originality but does gain credit for being one of the longer-standing institutions in town – and for doing precisely what it says on the tin. Descend a spiral staircase into a

warm and intimate basement, where you are presented with a long wooden bar, behind which efficient young men shake and stir as if their lives depend on it for a clientele that mixes loyal locals with visitors. As well as housing one of the best whisky collections in Prague, Alcohol Bar certainly doesn't shirk on the cocktail list – and it also has a humidor. The atmosphere is more gentlemen's club than Czech pub, and on the right night can be just as much fun as any other place in the area. If you don't know what to choose, ask for the Rum & Ginger cocktail – it's the house speciality.

Bar and Books, Týnská 19, Staré Město

Tel: 244 808 250 www.barandbooks.cz
Open: daily, 5pm–3am

Owned by the same crowd as the bars of the same name in New York, Prague's brand new Bar and Books is every bit as seductive and sophisticated as its Lexington and Hudson counterparts. Týnská is one of the city's cuter back streets, and this small bar fits in perfectly; candles are usually flickering outside, drawing you towards a mysterious, darkened interior – it's

almost impossible to walk past without wanting to find out more. Once you've pushed back the heavy velvet curtains you'll find yourself in a tiny, dark and delightfully upmarket cocktail bar, greeted by professional, well-dressed staff (including a bartender in a tux) and introduced to a fantastic drinks list that includes Martinis, brandies, whiskies, wines, cocktails and cigars. There's no real food on offer, but instead an incredibly intimate atmosphere that is just as perfect for pre- or post-dinner drinks as it is a premeditated charm offensive.

Blue Light, Josefská 1, Malá Strana
Tel: 257 533 126
Open: daily, 6pm–3am

With late opening hours, proximity to Charles Bridge (Malá Strana end) and a dark, cellar vibe (actually almost pitch black, illuminated only by lamps and candles, even though it's at street level), the Blue Light makes a great spot to enjoy some evening drinks. Characterized by seriously graffitied walls bearing an array of tortured posters featuring jazz legends like Ornette Coleman, and a jumbled assortment of battered leather sofas, wooden chairs and old shipping crates for tables, it's not necessarily a place for post-work Martinis; that said, it does have a mean and reasonably priced cocktail list and the jazz-Latin-Broadway-funk soundtrack (all on CD, no live acts) lends the place a fairly sophisticated air.

Bombay Cocktail Bar, Dlouhá 13, Josefov
Tel: 222 328 400
Open: daily, 6pm–3am (4am Fri–Sat)

One of the major cocktail players in the 'Triangle of Sin', Bombay (upstairs from the Rasoi Indian restaurant) has made significant strides towards becoming more chichi in recent years. Gone is the coloured crayon drinks list previously plastered all over the mirror behind the bar; in its stead are elegantly bound cocktail menus attracting a correspondingly 'together' clientele. Still, leopards don't change their spots all that quickly, and even though the drinks list stretches towards, well, oblivion, and the interior includes exposed brickwork, the music policy remains clichéd and the crowds are a shade less sophisticated than at nearby Tretters (see page 121). The foreign contingent is strong here, often hunting in packs; at weekends this is

a guaranteed place to find a crowded, buzzing atmosphere fuelled by pretty people, strong booze and euro-pop. If there's such a thing as a meat upmarket, Bombay may well be it.

Bugsy's, Pařížská 10, Josefov

Tel: 222 329 943 www.bugsysbar.cz

Open: daily, 7pm–2am

One of the grandes dames of Prague's burgeoning nightlife scene, and also one of its three premier cocktail establishments, Bugsy's has lost some of its

legendary exclusivity as nearby competitors have opened up. This location still pulls in the crowds, however, especially after a recent renovation pushed it forwards in terms of décor, style and feel. The 1950s themes have been toned down, but the award-winning bartenders still sport bow ties and braces and the disproportionately long bar is home to more liquor than you're likely to see in a while. Bugsy's also still makes some of the best cocktails in town and the location is great – since it's just a few steps from the seriously expensive and fashionable shops of Pařížská, the smart and the fashionable tend to drop by for an early evening aperitif while businessmen, locals and affluent tourists sup to the sounds of live music later on. At weekends, Bugsy's is almost always busy, so arrive early to get a good seat.

Duende, Karolíny Světlé 30, Staré Město

Tel: 222 221 255 www.duende.cz

Open: daily, 11am (5pm Sun)–1am

Located on the vaguely fashionable Karolíny Světlé (parallel to the river, close to Charles Bridge), Duende is a funky bohemian and unpretentious place that reveals its eclectic essence via jumbled knick-knack chic: tennis rackets, lamps, photos, old telephones, etc. The staff are as friendly and

down-to-earth as their regular clientele, who happen to be an assortment of locals and ex-pats that are every bit as varied as the decoration; everyone from minor celebrities to tourists, businessmen and students are wooed by the inclusive cosiness of Duende's enticing atmosphere. The location can get busy, but never seems overly crowded, making it a good option for an informal evening drink and chat. Friday nights sometimes offer live music, featuring a virtuoso Russian playing a mandolin.

Inn Ox Bar, Carlo IV, Senovážné Náměstí 13, Nové Město
Tel: 224 593 090 www.boscolohotels.com
Open: daily, 10am–2am

The bar at the Carlo IV (see Sleep) is one of the most stylish locations in Prague. Designed by Adam D. Tihany, this space would effortlessly embellish any hotel in London, Paris or New York. A long, central bar dominates the room; finished in back-lit glass and steel, this slice of style is a masterpiece of grace and design, forming an illumined centrepiece to the rest of the glamorous interior. Long white curtains billow over the windows while an

elite coterie of residents and guests sip exquisitely prepared cocktails. There's a cigar bar on the other side of the lobby, which is housed in the old vaults of the bank, existing as a separate entity. Dark and intimate, Inn Ox is the perfect place for an after-dinner glass of brandy. You might even be sufficiently seduced by your surroundings to stay for a second round.

Kozička, Kozí 1, Josefov
Tel: 224 818 308 www.kozicka.cz
Open: daily, noon–4am

Kozička ('Little Goat') is a typical Czech basement bar, playing host to some tourists and ex-pats but mainly catering to locals. Internally, it's not particularly impressive, nor does it really have the ambience of anything other than

a good neighbourhood bar, despite being just off Old Town Square. Brick walls and basic wooden furniture sum up Kozička's simplicity and homeliness, but there almost always seems to be a pair of attractive Czech girls pouting in the corner, expertly sidestepping the advances of hopeful foreigners. The bar staff are suitably blunt, the food reassuringly average, and the beer refreshingly cheap for the area. If you're feeling in need of a break from fancier places, this may be just what you're looking for.

KU Café, Rytířská 13, Staré Město
Tel: 221 181 081
Open: daily, 2pm–2am

K.U. (for 'Kent Universe') Café was once one of Prague's hippest bars. Its status has slipped somewhat in recent years, but it's still one of the premier nightspots to see and be seen in. Tucked in between Old Town Square and Wenceslas Square (just opposite its sister venue, Café Café), KU Café's

location might be central but it feels far removed from the madding crowds that can flood the main arteries of the city. The clientele seem to be drawn directly from the social pages and gossip sections of the local press, and eye each other up and down to the repetitive throb of house music. The refined selection of cocktails – well proportioned, nicely mixed, just like the tunes – lubricate the masses. The more these hipsters sip, the more their lipstick slips and the music gets louder until – eventually – it can all turn into quite good fun.

Legends, Týn 1, Staré Město
Tel: 224 895 404 www.legends.cz
Open: daily, 10am–1am (4am Fri–Sat)

This is a key Prague venue for sports lovers. If there's an important football, rugby or boxing match taking place, you can guarantee Legends will be showing it on their 20 or more screens. Ostensibly a revamped brick cellar bar, the main room is long and slender with rows of televisions along each wall and a large screen at one end. There are tables under the screens, as well as a large central island you can sit around and watch several matches at the same time. You're unlikely to come across many locals here, as it's more of an ex-pat and tourist hang-out; and yes, it gets raucous and drunken, especially on big match days. But most of the time Legends is a regular

bar with a sporty theme, supplying not only beer but also a decent selection of food, friendly service and a respectable clientele.

M1, Masná 1, Josefov
Tel: 221 874 256
Open: daily, 6pm–4am

A relatively new bar in the middle of the 'Triangle of Sin', M1 has a strong industrial feel, complete with concrete floors, a metal bar and large, loft-

style windows. The hard lines are slightly softened by red velvet banquettes that run along the walls; small stainless-steel tables are placed at regular intervals and large mirrors at each end help to increase the feeling of space. This is one of the few bars in the area that actually makes an effort with its music policy. The various sounds pumping from the system each night include house, indie rock, hip hop/R&B and drum & bass, all mixed to near-perfection by a solid range of local DJs. During the week M1 is a great place to meet and chat; at weekends this space is as busy as the eponymous British motorway on a bank-holiday weekend, crammed with young, trendy Czechs and ex-pats. There's talk of a major upscale overhaul, but for now the old school vibe remains refreshingly intact.

Monarch Wine Bar, Na Perštýně 15, Staré Město

Tel: 224 23 96 02 www.monarchvinnysklep.cz
Open: 11am–11pm. Closed Sundays.

Monarch is a fairly central and unpretentious wine bar connected to a wine shop, and easily found thanks to the neon green strip-lights that frame the entrance. The main room is large and comfortable; the large windows allow for good people-watching and give the space a light, airy feel. Plenty of room is afforded between tables, and an enticing bar runs across one side of the space. The cavernous stone cellar below houses an enormous selection of wines that stretches to over 1,000 vintages, and includes choices from virtually all European and New World countries as well as a solid range of Czech and Moravian varieties. Indulgences don't end with the wine, as Monarch

also boasts a well-stocked humidor and speciality snacks. Check the blackboard indicating the daily deli selections, normally featuring a few French and Swiss cheeses, fondue, sausages and paté. By-the-glass prices are convenient for connoisseurs and modest tipplers alike, and the renovated cellar can be reserved for group tasting events (complete with your own sommelier). Since the place closes around 10pm or so, it's best used as a pre-dinner spot or for a relaxed evening drink.

Ocean Drive, V Kolkovně 7, Josefov

Tel: 224 819 089 www.tretters.cz

Open: daily, 11am–2am

The younger sibling of Tretters, Ocean Drive has given a dash of additional glamour to the 'Triangle of Sin'. Where Tretters is downtown NYC, OD is pure South Beach, Miami: extravagant, upbeat and, admittedly, a little surreal

in the middle of grey Prague. Among the assorted decorations live a piano, a large mural, LCD screens, red leather banquettes and photos personifying a carefree life on the coast. More important is the attractive, well-stocked bar, which offers the mandatory cast of cocktails, wines, beers and mixers. Like Tretters, its more low-key neighbour, Ocean Drive attracts quite a few 30-something Czechs and flush tourists, successfully building on the chain's reputation to provide an exclusive and decadent retreat for some of Prague's more affluent residents.

St Nicholas' Café, Tržiště 10, Malá Strana

Tel: 257 530 205

Open: daily, noon–midnight (3am Fri–Sat)

One of the more relaxed places to come for an evening drink, and one of the few hip spots on 'the other side' of the river, St Nicholas' Café is not really a café at all but a low-key cellar bar that draws a good spread of students, ex-pats and urban sophisticates. The host building is listed (UNESCO) and dates all the way back to 1554. The low-vaulted ceilings, cosy nooks and low lighting create a seductively snug ambience, enhanced by the friendly bar staff and the occasional live band. It's often quite busy for drinks and dinner (the pizzas are also good if that's all you fancy) but if by chance the

setting is too quiet for you, and you don't feel like wandering too far, you can always pop down the road to the slightly more boisterous jazz venue U Malého Glena (see Party).

Techtle Mechtle, Vinohradská 47, Vinohrady
Tel: 222 250 143   www.techtle-mechtle.cz
Open: daily, 5pm–4am

Techtle Mechtle ('Hanky Panky') is one of Prague's newest and hottest nightspots. A restaurant-club-bar complex located beneath street level (in a cellar allegedly accidentally bombed by a rogue US missile in 1945), it has an all-in-one feel that is just as comprehensive as it is self-conscious. Unlike many basement venues, Techtle Mechtle offers generous amounts of space within its vaulted ceilings and exposed brick walls. The priorities of the place can be easily determined by comparing the fairly limited, Italian-based menu

with the infinitely weightier cocktail list. Nevertheless, the food is pretty good, and since it's a little out of the way the fact that the kitchen is open until 2am is very convenient. The real reason to come here, however, is either to nod along to the DJ beats in the main room, or to sit in a dark corner of the cocktail bar and indulge in the very activities that the venue's name suggests.

Tom Tom Club, Dlouhá 46, Josefov
Tel: 224 828 374 tomtomclub@volny.cz
Open: daily, 10am–1am

The Tom Tom Club were a new wave band from the States, who once wrote a song called 'Booming and Zooming'; in that song they used the word 'defenestration', which means, essentially, the act of launching someone out of a window. Prague is famous for its history of defenestrations, and it also

has a bar called the Tom Tom Club. Make of this what you will. It is all lost, of course, on the chilled clientele of this laid-back and dimly lit bar on the busy street of Dlouhá. It's an eternally popular hang-out that boasts walls painted in vogue-ish (and vampish) blood-red, distinctive ornamentation (especially in the back room) and furnishings that favour simplicity over style. The inhabitants, mainly Czech, are a young and trendy crowd who come to drink, chat and smoke rather than shout, pose and jostle. It makes for a relaxed counterpoint to many of the loud and bustling bars in the area, and is ideal for a drink before you head off to the Roxy, which is just over the road.

Tretters, V Kolkovně 3, Josefov
Tel: 224 811 165 www.tretters.cz
Open: daily, 7pm–3am

Suited and booted gents sip cocktails while elegant ladies preen and perch on bar stools – if Prague nightlife were a film, Tretters would probably be the main set. Although it's one of the primary hang-outs for Prague's exclusive and wannabe glam set, the actual space is nonetheless surprisingly mellow, mixing excellent cocktails with fairly naff music and serving them in convivial ambience. A burly doorman acts as an effective filter after 8pm, meaning once in you are safe from the plebeian masses (stag groups, that is).

An extensive list of cocktails is contained within a hard-backed tome found on the bar – more than enough to keep you busy for an entire weekend. The uniformed bar staff are smart and efficient, and do amazingly well to cope with the constant demands at peak periods given how time-consuming it can be to churn out such delicately made drinks. Tretters is the kind of place where you might meet the long-limbed model of your dreams, although our survey suggests you will need to be either well dressed or obviously wealthy (or both) before you receive much attention.

Ultramarin, Ostrovní 32, Nové Město
Tel: 224 932 249 www.ultramarin.cz
Open: daily, 11am–4am

In Prague, customers just tend to leave if there aren't seats available – they don't stand around. Hence popular spots, such as this attractive grill-bar/music-club on the edge of SoNa, are often extended in order to cope with the ever-increasing influx. Ultramarin might not be as modern or chic as some of the bars and restaurants in the Old Town area but it does offer a buzzing vibe and a friendly crowd. Frequented by young, predominantly Czech folk, the kitchen produces tasty food well into the early hours – which is just as well, since downstairs in the basement lurks a club that can

get pretty rau-
cous. The red-
bricked high ceil-
ings of the main
room also frame a
great space for
relaxed late-night
drinking, so if you
want to remain
distinctly chilled,
stay upstairs; if
you're looking for

adventure, then slip into Ultramarin's darker depths.

Zvonařka, Šafaříkova 1, Vinohrady
Tel: 224 251 990 www.zvonarka.cz
Open: daily, 11am–2am (midnight Sunday)

A wannabe cool bar-restaurant in the heart of Vinohrady, Zvonařka is built
from glass, steel, neon and wood, elements that have been combined to create a modern space that favours simple, clean, modern lines. There is a separate bar, restaurant and lounge area, but the large outdoor terrace offering

panoramic views over the city's southern reaches is the real reason to head
out here. Zvonařka is known to host
some of the best private parties in
town, so if you're able to crash one,
consider yourself a legend; otherwise,
they still have Prague's finest DJs spin-
ning the decks at weekends. The
restaurant is reasonable but its
Mexican/Asian/Czech food is nothing
to shout from the terrace about.
Zvonařka is worth a visit if you're
staying in this part of town, but check
ahead for events if you're coming from
the centre since it's not always a
buzzing place.

snack...

Prague's coffee-house traditions stretch back to the beginning of the 18th century, when Georgius Deodatus, a trader from Damascus, opened the first café over in Malá Strana. Ever since, café culture has been an increasingly important aspect of Prague social life.

While traditional Czech pubs, with their drab, smoky surroundings and masculine leanings, are often uninviting for women, modern cafés can provide more sophisticated and gender-friendly atmospheres, yet at the same time still offer alcohol and substantial meals as well as snacks, coffee and tea.

There are two sorts of café we recommend in Prague: smart and chic, and traditional and cosy. Traditional spots might be shrouded in smoke, but the ones we have selected serve decent, hearty food and an array of local wines. Frequented by locals and the occasional tourist, they are welcoming and friendly.

One unusual phenomenon in Prague café culture is the prominence of the tea house; this serves rare and delicate teas from around the world in peaceful and relaxing surroundings. Dobrá Cajovna and Dahab (below) offer tranquillity,

space and a mind-boggling range of teas.

By far the biggest vogue in Prague, however, is for cooler cafés (such as Café Café – right), which cater for more well-heeled crowds: glamorous locals, affluent expats and switched-on tourists. These upmarket spots offer delicious food, calorie-laden cakes and 'real' coffee – as well as non-smoking areas. A couple of the cafés we have listed serve delicious gourmet food but cious gourmet food but have not been classified as restaurants because of their limited capacity and/or suitability for daytime dining: Café-Flambée, Sovovy Mlyny and U Zajove are examples. Others, such as Au Gourmand, don't serve meals at all, but specialize in heavenly cakes and devilish puddings.

Cafés are generally cheaper than restaurants but a little more expensive than pubs. It's unusual to pay much more than 40kc for a glass of wine or beer and 120kc for a plate of food.

As well as cafés, we have listed a few restaurants that offer good lunch deals; the Lemon Leaf and Siam I San offer delicious Thai food while if you're in the mood for some Lebanese *mezze*, Dahab is very good indeed.

Au Gourmand, Dlouhá 10, Staré Město

Tel: 222 329 060
Open: daily, 9am–7pm

A former butcher's shop behind Old Town Square, Au Gourmand has been elegantly transformed into a French-style patisserie. The room, still tiled from the days of its former incarnation, has two counters serving a stunning

array of cakes, desserts and a selection of delicious tarts and sandwiches. Everything is clean and fresh, almost to the point of sterility. At the back, there's a second small room with leather banquettes where you can get stuck into some seriously sticky slices away from the envious, prying eyes of passers-by. A deli section provides gourmet food and wine to take away. Great for a quick bite on the move or a cup of tea and something sweet.

Café Café, Rytířská 10, Staré Město

Tel: 224 210 597 www.cafe-cafe.cz
Open: daily, 10am (11am Sat–Sun)–midnight

You can practically smell the sassiness in Café Café – an unapologetically modern and spacious place with tall windows that allow premium ogling both sides of the glass, large mirrors that host wafer-thin LCD screens, and 'Pretty Young Things' who sashay between the tables with studied aloofness. The café offers a satisfying range of 21st-century teas, infusions and coffees, as well as a small but trendy continental menu with pastas, risottos, salads and the like. Situated between Wenceslas Square and Old Town Square, the location is central without being overrun by gaggles of tourists. Whether

you're sipping a coffee on the terrace in the summer or huddling into its funky embrace in colder weather, Café Café is an accessible and enjoyable spot for people-watching, chatting and snacking.

Café Carolina, Nerudova 44, Hradčany
Tel: 257 535 557 www.hotelneruda-praha.cz
Open: daily, 7am–11pm

Attached to snazzy design hotel Neruda (see Sleep), Café Carolina provides

a chic rest-stop as you negotiate the long road up towards the Castle. The elegant, contemporary room, with its large, street-facing windows and affable cream and beige hues, is actually part of a larger hotel restaurant (complete with glass atrium and outdoor terrace), but nevertheless makes a delightful spot to pause and recharge the batteries. The main menu offers tasty Czech food, but you can also order coffees and cakes, sandwiches and soups, and – calorie count permitting – the café speciality: an industrial-strength hot chocolate.

Café Flambée, Husova 5, Staré Město
Tel: 224 401 236 www.flambee.cz
Open: daily, 11am–11pm

A dashing, graceful café in the very heart of the Old Town, Café Flambée is the sibling bistro of the expensive, more formal restaurant of the same name. The crisp white tablecloths, comfy red chairs, pine floor and soft lighting lend it an exclusive and intimate atmosphere, while the strip mirrors on the wall and the stainless-steel bar add a dash of modern sophistication. The

innovative menu is divided into contemporary Czech food, several vegetarian options and modern world cuisine, all complemented, of course, by a delicious dessert menu and some great wines. The food here is deservedly renowned, and the café successfully caters to a clientele in search of a more discerning venue. It also offers a decent alternative to the restaurant downstairs when the latter is fully booked.

Café Indigo, Platnéřská 11, Staré Město
Tel: 731 216 035 www.indigospace.cz
Open: daily, 9am–midnight

Café Indigo is a large, industrial space housed in an old building that flanks one side of the Klementinum, near Charles Bridge. Presenting a mix of decorative styles – simple wooden chairs with stainless-steel tables, an industrial steel bar, angular sculptures and odd artwork – it's very 'avant-prague', although some of its design elements date back 30 years. The large dimensions and arty (rather than chic) décor give the place an intellectual feel, and indeed it's more popular with students and locals than tourists. That said, it's friendly enough and the lack of pretension can be refreshing after you've experienced some of

the city's cooler hotspots. The menu, which consists of steady Czech options, won't bowl you over, but it is cheap, and you can get a decent beer or glass of wine. A good place for a quiet lunch or a quick beer, or for reading an existentialist novel with a glass of Moravian wine.

Café Louvre, Národní třída 20, Nové Město
Tel: 224 930 949 www.kavarny.cz/louvre
Open: daily, 8am–11.30pm

One of Prague's most seasoned institutions, Café Louvre – which first opened in 1902 – is a must-lunch place. Even if you're not a fan of cafés, the building is a masterpiece of Art Deco reconstruction, with huge ceilings punctuated by chandeliers, outsized paintings on the walls and staff dressed in traditional uniform. There's even a good-sized billiard room out back, in tribute to the café's original turn-of-the-century leisure ideals. Ostensibly a

series of different rooms (including a modern art café on the way up the stairs), the café offers a classic range of Czech, French and continental dishes – avoid the pedestrian pastas and aim for the hearty meat dishes. Café Louvre is a splendid place to take breakfast, with a variety of set menus themed by nationality (American, French, English, etc.), and a memorable lunch spot too. Kafka spent 'lovely, gentle hours' here; ex-pats (there are free English newspapers), locals and tourists still do today.

Café Montmartre, Řetězová 7, Staré Město
Tel: 222 221 143
Open: daily, 10am–6pm

Café Montmartre is a genuine reconstruction of the famed original, which operated between 1911 and 1937 and was immensely popular with the city's demi-monde and literati (Jaroslav Hasek was a regular; but then he

was a regular in pretty much all of the city's bars). With the original immortalized in the city's literature, this modern version revisits the shabby charm of its predecessor (where Egon Kisch famously danced with Anna Cacka), complete with battered sofas and scarred tables, antique lamps and black-and-white photos of former patrons, all under a barrel-vaulted, painted ceiling. The scruffiness is part of its appeal, and although the corner piano remains silent these days, Montmartre is popular most evenings, when an eclectic assortment of customers gather to natter over coffee and wine.

Café Savoy, Vitězná 5, Malá Strana
Tel: 257 311 562 www.ambi.cz
Open: daily, 8am (9am Sat–Sun)–10.30pm

Café Savoy, located across the river from the National Theatre, was once
the kind of turn-of-the-century coffee house popular with subversive revo-
lutionary types. Modernized first of all in 2001, it has recently been given an
Art Nouveau makeover by its new owners, the local Ambiente chain. Today

the Savoy makes for a very welcoming and comfortable locale, with its nostalgic period detailing: chandeliers, restored *trompe l'oeil* ceiling and replica
railings. The menu features all you need for a fulfilling café stop – teas, coffees and chocolates, snacks, sandwiches and soups, as well as larger options
that favour heavy Czech and French cuisine. There's also a small but considered wine list with German, French and Italian varieties.

Café Slavia, Smetanovo Nábřeži 2, Staré Město
Tel: 224 218 493
Open: daily, 9am–midnight

This large café on the riverbank is another of Prague's venerable institutions. Situated next to the National Theatre, Slavia was once host to Czech
playwrights and political subversives (supposedly, Apollinaire used to sup
absinthe here). These days it serves as a rather more sedate example of Art
Deco nostalgia, although – along with the Theatre across the road – it maintains a definite nationalist aura. In addition to the wonderfully retro surroundings, Slavia offers comfortable seating, large windows that boast

superb views of the Castle and Charles Bridge (if you're quick or early enough to grab a table next to one), and a robust, if slightly predictable, menu that features pancakes, pastas and similar fare. True, it's mainly popular with tourists, but the space is large enough to ensure that the café does not compromise on intimacy.

Cukr Káva Limonáda, Lázeňská 7, Malá Strana
Tel: 257 530 628
Open: daily, 8am–11pm

It's hard to believe that such a sophisticated little spot could exist so close to the brash tourist traps of the Royal Way, but Cukr Káva Limonáda is precisely that. It's a small space but immediately welcoming, with simple wooden furnishings, florally decorated ceiling and crisply linear aesthetic. Young,

friendly staff busy themselves with a diverse clientele, serving up everything from hearty designer breakfasts (scrambled eggs with Burgundy ham), ciabattas and lunches to moreish macchiatos, wine, soups and yummy cakes. The regular menu is diverse, and there are also daily specials marked in large letters on the blackboard, as well as a discerning wine list. The owners are trying to introduce midweek film nights in the evenings, but for now it remains more of a lunchtime spot. Glass aficionados might be interested in the showroom next door.

Dahab, Dlouhá 33, Josefov
Tel: 221 827 375   www.dahab.cz
Open: daily, noon–1am

Founded by Prague's 'king of tea', Lubos Rychvalsk, who introduced Prague to Eastern tea cultures following the 1989 revolution, Dahab is a Moroccan

tearoom and *mezze* restaurant that combines an ethnic funkiness with a sedate, laid-back atmosphere. It's the essence of what an Arab tearoom should be: pink vaulting supports a sky-blue ceiling, mosaic counters hide Arabian delicacies and waiters scurry about with hookah pipes while chilled music adds an extra touch of serenity. Persian carpets and cushions set in front of traditional tables accommodate a mixture of loyal Czechs, young ex-pats and the occasional tourist. The Lebanese menu offers a choice of savouries, starters and *mezze*, plus a wide selection of teas, coffees and cocktails; *tajines* and couscous dishes are also available. Everything is reasonably priced and the food good, making this a great place to unwind. If only it offered massages as well...

Dinitz Café, Na Poříčí 12, Staré Město

Tel: 222 314 071   www.dinitz.cz
Open: daily, 8am–3am

The sleek, Art Deco charms of Dinitz have been something of a local secret for the last couple of years – not only because of its slightly tucked-away location (although that hasn't helped) but also because the road it's on was plagued by construction for a long while and people generally gave it a wide berth. Things are different now, however, and the café-bar is finally getting the attention it deserves. The lush black interior, which immediately transports you back some 70 years, makes a tasteful – and tasty – spot for breakfasts as well as lunches. The menu is interesting and varied, ranging from sandwiches and salads to *goulashes*,  *risotti* and meat dishes, all well executed. Come in the evening the place is transformed into a live music venue, and the sumptuous cocktail and whisky bar comes into its own.

Divini's, Týnska 23, Staré Město

Tel: 224 808 318   www.divinis.cz
Open: 11am–4pm, 6pm–midnight

Originally a wine shop, this snug little restaurant is rapidly drawing in the great and the good for its excellent Italian food and fine selection of Tuscan, Sicilian and other wines. A short but frequently changing menu offers original and interesting dishes executed with fresh ingredients and an attractive simplicity. The Italian owner is often in attendance, giving advice on choosing wines and engaging the clientele in long, animated conversations. The staff are Italian too and, surprise, surprise, also love a good chat – let's just say that the amiable ambience means the food can sometimes take a while to arrive. Not that you'll mind. You'll be far too relaxed and at home even to notice, and when the Florentine steak or white truffle dishes arrive you'll be glad you came. Excellent

for romantic lunches or intimate evening meals.

Dobrá Čajovna, Václavské Náměstí 14, Nové Město
Tel: 224 231 480 www.cajovna.com
Open: daily, 11am (2pm Sun)–9.30pm

Hidden in a little courtyard just off Wenceslas Square, this is easily one of the best tea houses in Prague. The exterior is inconspicuous, but pass through the gates and courtyard, and you'll enter a spotlessly clean, dimly lit room dotted with people chatting away or quietly lost in books. Ambient, nu-age tunes wash over the clientele, creating a reasonably surreal setting when contrasted with the cacophony of the square outside. Mobile phones and smoking are banned to maintain the purity, and the tea menu stretches on for an eternity. The choice is spectacular – teas from the Americas, Africa and the East; white teas, green teas, black teas, red teas – all presented in a

huge book and featuring wry, in-depth descriptions. Once you've chosen, ring the itsy bell on your tea-crate table and the waiter will appear to take your order. Feeling peckish? The menu stretches Middle-Eastern style dips and breads, although the kitchen can rustle up bigger portions on request. If you feel like kicking off your shoes and sipping something refreshing while reading a book or having a calm chat, this is one of the best places in Prague to do it.

Dolce Vita, Siroká 15, Josefov
Tel: 222 329 192
Open: daily, 8am–midnight

A small, hip Italian café found just around the corner from the main designer shopping avenue of Pařížská, Dolce Vita (there are no Fellini connections) is part *gelateria*-cake shop, part café-wine bar. It stocks a hugely tempting selection of calorie-laden pastries, cakes and Italian ice cream, which you can take away or eat while watching the shoppers struggle by under the weight

of their Dunhill and Hermès bags. The neat interior and smartly decked-out tables encourage a longer stay, and if you do drop your bags and sit down you won't be disappointed. Not only are the coffees and snacks superlatively good, but the breakfasts are also great and, for later visitors, there is a very decent wine and champagne list. An upstairs gallery area provides a little extra privacy, although cafés don't really get much more intimate than this in any case.

Fischer Café, Jakubská 6, Staré Město
Tel: 222 321 386   www.fischercafe.cz
Open: 8am–11pm Mon–Fri; 9am–noon Sat–Sun

This smartly appointed café is found just behind Tyn Church, just a couple of back streets from Old Town Square. The pleasant interior, all crisp white chairs and tables, trendy travel photos on the walls and a natty Italian cof-

fee/drinks bar, is immediately appealing – more so even than the smarter but more formal restaurant downstairs. Service is as swift and casual as the décor suggests, and the menu, while not overly imaginative, serves decent pastas, fish and meat dishes, as well as some Italian-style specialities. While the food is good, however, it's not mind-blowing, and Fischer's prices can seem somewhat ambitious. It may be best, in other words, to save that relaxed three-course dream for another spot.

Globe, Pštrossova 6, Nové Město
Tel: 224 934 203 www.globebookstore.cz
Open: daily, 10am–midnight (1am Sat–Sun)

Part internet café, part bookstore, part café, the Globe is the main hang-out for the American student fraternity, but it also provides a nerve-centre for all students and ex-pats – a place where they can feel at home among hot-mail addresses and English language newspapers. Staff are young and friendly, and the food is… is… well, it's okay. There are cheap breakfast, lunch and dinner menus as well as à la carte options, but the brownies, lattes and ambience are the main attraction. It's a popular WiFi spot (1kc per minute),

so don't be sur-
prised to find
half the clientele
lost in cyber-
space during the
day. Come
evening, there is
often live enter-
tainment in the
form of book
readings, art
exhibitions and

live music; since there's a range of alcoholic drinks available, it's worth bearing in mind for an evening out. The well-stocked bookshop offers essential
Czech classics as well as good international selections (all in English) and
tome-buyers are rewarded with WiFi credit.

Kavarná Obecní Dům, Náměstí Republiky 5, Staré Město
Tel: 222 002 770   www.obecnidum.cz
Open: daily, 11am–11pm

This huge Art Deco room – which dates back to 1912, and boasts fantastic
chandeliers and beautiful wall-mounted light brackets – is home to Prague's
most ornate and opulent café and Pilsen restaurant. Large windows look

out on to the Námestí
Republiky, where
tourists mill around and
costumed concert-
ticket sellers tout their
goods. In the summer,
there's terrace seating
outside to take full
advantage of the
Continental warmth. A
fairly unexciting menu
of café dishes (salads,
sandwiches and
desserts) is on offer,

although you may like to note that it's one of the few spots where you can get scrambled eggs and meats on Sundays. As you might expect, dining in such a recherché setting has a price, but it's still reasonable by British standards, and the surroundings alone make it worthwhile – it's simply too stunning not to stop in for a quick bite or glass of beer. The entrance is through the equally impressive Municipal House.

Lemon Leaf, Na Zderaze 14, Nové Město
Tel: 224 919 056 www.lemon.cz
Open: daily, 11am–11pm

While the number of people throwing sushi down their necks in Prague continues to grow at exponential rates, finding a decent Thai meal is still conspicuously hard work. Just a little way along from Karlovo Náměstí (a stone's throw from the Globe café), the Lemon Leaf is one of the city's better stop-offs for a decent *pad thai*. The interior is large and sparsely deco-

rated but the pleasant bar and buzzing atmosphere lend the place a casual, vibrant feel. The menu mixes Thai specialities with steaks, pasta, salads and vegetarian dishes. Each day there's a different set lunch menu and buffet (but note that at weekends the latter gets depleted somewhat swiftly). Haute cuisine 'tis not, but the spice factor is high, the prices are good and most of the Thai dishes are very tasty indeed.

Lobkowicz Palace Café, Jiřská 3, Hradčany
Tel: 602 595 998 www.lobkowiczevents.cz
Open: daily, 10am–6pm

Since it was returned to the Lobkowicz family in 2003, the Lobkowicz
Palace has been leased to the Czech National Museum. In the adjacent
building the café-restaurant and terrace have reopened, and with a
panoramic view of Prague, freshly made lunches and regal ambience, this is
one of the more enjoyable spots in the Castle area to grab a coffee or a

snack. The interior, although not huge, is nicely decorated with high-backed
chairs and neutral tones. The terrace is the spot to head for, incredibly
romantic in summer and even enjoyable in winter thanks to the blankets
and heat lamps laid on by the attentive staff. The ceiling mural in the café
proper alludes to the old Lobkowicz tradition of making beers (since 1466)
and fine wines (since 1603), both of which are also on sale here should you
need some Dutch courage for the trek back home.

Noodles, Politických vězňů 12, Nové Město
Tel: 234 100 110 www.hotel-yasmin.cz
Open: daily, noon–midnight

If pasta's your thing, then Noodles, which features pastas from all over the
globe – from Italy to Indonesia, Mongolia to Thailand – is your place. If you
like to dine in designer surroundings, even better, since Noodles is the asso-
ciate restaurant of trendy Hotel Yasmin (see Sleep) and offers, along with
good food, a highly memorable interior. While many hotel restaurants are

(frankly) quite stuffy, Noodles creates an ambience that, while complementary to the Yasmin, is also distinct from it. It's separated by a lengthy corridor (where you can also sit and take a coffee), and instead of the hotel's olive-green leaf motif, Noodles occupies a red cram and chrome world of its own that's all mirror-ball lights, tufty red installations sprouting from the floor, and a variety of table/chair/booth/stool combinations. There's even a separate entrance, making it conveniently

accessible from Wenceslas Square. You would almost expect mediocre food in such a striking environment, but Noodles manages to deliver on pretty much all counts.

Le Patio, Národní 22, Nové Město
Tel: 224 918 072 www.patium.com
Open: daily, 8am (11am Sun)–11pm

Le Patio is a haven of tranquillity in the midst of the hustle and bustle of

busy Národní. Inside the double doors lies something resembling a magical-realist fantasy: a high-ceilinged room bedecked with Arab lanterns, a ship's bow, eye-catching furnishings imported from afar. If you hadn't thought of travelling somewhere distant and exotic before entering, you may well do once inside. Chilled ambient/world music distracts you further from the trams rumbling past outside and the menu provides French and oriental dishes with an emphasis on healthy salads and couscous dishes. It's just right for a break from shopping; then again, the large shop out the back stocks a fantastic range of imported furniture and knick-knacks, so it's also good for shopping too.

Radost FX Café, Běleradská 120, Vinohrady
Tel: 224 254 776 www.radostfx.cz
Open: daily, 11am–5am

The Radost FX empire is legendary – not only in Prague but also across Europe, since London's Ministry of Sound rated it one of the top 20 clubs in the world. The café section occupying a quarter of the building has long been an institution for Prague's young and style-conscious as a hang-out and

meeting-place. The furniture is mock-classical, with comfortable banquettes, wrought-iron chairs and distressed tables, while in the larger rooms at the rear you get to lounge on deep sofas and chill to post-club sounds. It's unashamedly cool at all hours. A long cocktail list ensures its popularity with the chic post-work crowd, and once the club beneath is in full swing, the café doubles up as a chill-out zone. Always busy, it's also noted for its fine and suitably adventurous vegetarian fare. Best of all, it continues to serve food until the smallest hours of the morning.

Sahara Café, Ibsenova 1, Vinohrady
Tel: 222 514 987
Open: 8am–midnight Mon–Sat; 11am–11pm Sun

With its exquisite (and exotic) sandy-coloured interior, large windows that look onto a leafy square and wonderfully sedate, oriental atmosphere,

Sahara is well worth the trip out to Vinohrady. Relax among soft cushions in the spacious anteroom, or pass beyond to find a series of rooms and areas separated by imported antiques and fabrics, but in hot weather aim for the garden. Sahara's forte is its attention to detail, but not only with the décor – the breakfast and lunch menus, which offer a pleasant range of morning fare (*croissants*, pastries, coffees), plus fuller meals that include Argentinian meats, fish dishes, couscous and Italian classics – all made with authentic imported ingredients and presented pretty much to perfection. If only all cafés were this good.

Siam I San, Valentinská 11, Josefov
Tel: 224 814 099   www.arzenal.cz
Open: daily, 10am–midnight

It won't be the best Thai you'll ever eat, but it will probably be the first time you've had Thai food at the back of a glassware gallery. Borek Sipek is best known as a world-class glass designer, whose works can be found in major museums in Europe, Japan, America and elsewhere. This space, just around the corner from the Rudolfinum, is first and foremost a gallery for his works, although once you've gawked at the glassy goods on offer (and their prices), you can pass through into the wholly unexpected Thai restaurant. Filled with a eclectic mix of designer glassware, kitsch tablecloths, elegant black-and-white photographs and Buddha heads, Siam I San is an esoteric space, but one that is popular with lunching locals and tourists alike. The

menu is typically Thai, with the staple dishes of *tom yum* soup, *pad Thai* and green curry on offer. The prices are reasonable (especially the weekend buffet lunch) and the ambience pleasant, but it's the fresh chilli (not so common in the Czech Republic) that really spices things up.

Sovový Mlýny, U Sovových Mlýnů, Malá Strana
Tel: 257 535 900 www.sovovymlyny.com
Open: daily, 9am–midnight

Located in the Kampa Museum of Modern Art, Sovovy is a small, refined and contemporary space. The café is split into two areas, with an outside terrace open in summer that enjoys splendid views over the Vltava towards the Old

Town. The simple décor is dotted with interesting pictures and objéts d'art, which provide the perfect backdrop to what is a fairly sophisticated menu. The dishes, which display a modern approach to Czech cooking, are just the right size to ensure that you can still manage to walk after lunch – perfect for those planning to look at the Museum (recommended). The food is delicious, and demonstrates a refreshing approach to local cuisine – Sovovy does what it feels is stylish without pandering to local 'authenticity'.

Ultramarin, Ostrovní 32, Nové Město

Tel: 224 932 249 www.ultramarin.cz
Open: daily, noon–3am

An attractive space located in the trendy SoNa district, Ultramarin serves as a café, evening bar, nightclub and restaurant. The food isn't bad at all, although perhaps it best serves as a hearty lunch rather than an evening meal. The menu is international, with Thai dishes, vegetarian options, Italian

and French dishes and a daily specials list. The atmosphere is generally young and vibrant, with a healthy mix of students, hipsters, business folk and locals occupying the heavy iron chairs and large wooden tables. There's generally local artwork and photographs on the walls and decent music on the stereo, plus a good wine list, should you wish to get settled in for the afternoon.

Universal, V Jirchářích 6, Nové Město

Tel: 224 934 416
Open: daily, 11am–1am

A bistro in the heart of SoNa, behind the National Theatre, Universal is an atmospheric little place with purposefully plain wooden tables and chairs and a bizarre array of decoration on the walls. A long French poem winds around the room, while a moulded elephant's head hangs near some traffic lights. So far, so atypical. Sadly the creativity stops at the menu, which is typi-

cally French/Italian and not particularly inventive. The service can be disappointingly indifferent, although on a good day waiters and chefs can come together to make a memorable lunchtime event. Since it's off the tourist track, at least it provides a quieter place to eat.

U Zavoje, Havelská 25, Staré Město

Tel: 226 006 120 www.uzavoje.cz
Open: daily, 11am–midnight

U Zavoje is an upmarket complex that occupies the best part of an old alley off Havelská, opposite the baroque church. There's a restaurant, a cheese shop, wine bar and a café; all are good but the café is probably your best bet. A natural, unostentatious space, it boasts lots of natural light, a cracking wine cellar and food that may well leave you reeling. The spread of business newspapers and financial magazines on the window ledge testifies to the kind of clientele that normally lunch at U Zajove – expense account diners and well heeled locals, mostly – but it's informal enough for anyone to eat here without feeling out of place. The menu offers classic French cooking (seafood, meats, foie gras) with delightfully innovative twists, while the wine list, like the menu, is limited but impeccable. The starters and desserts are usually as titillating as the mains, so plan for an extended lunch. Not cheap, but highly memorable.

U Zeleného Čaje, Nerudova 19, Hradčany
Tel: 257 530 027
Open: daily, 11am–10pm

This cosy tearoom provides a resting-place on the long, steep walk up the Royal Way towards the Castle. It serves a range of traditional and original brews, from Earl Grey to Mongolian Smoked. The warm and welcoming atmosphere is tinged with the pungent smell of incense, nu-age music and

simple, uncluttered décor. Staff are friendly and helpful, and although it's not quite as casual or chilled as other tearooms, it is quite sophisticated. It doubles as a shop, too, where you can buy a range of different teas and corresponding accessories. Sipping on a Brutal Nikita or a Tuareg brew while ordering a Hare Krishna burger might not be a quintessentially Czech experience, but it is most memorable, nevertheless.

party...

Nightlife in Prague is fun, safe and – with the exception of the occasional boisterous stag group – largely unthreatening. Unsurprisingly, the most prominent section of the city for making merry is the central Old Town area. The biggest concentration of tourist and ex-pat bars – cheesy and chic alike – are located here, making this district vibrant, but also more expensive, than other areas of the city.

You're unlikely to find many Czechs at play in the Old Town, although of course some will venture out to get down with the visiting masses. Venues such as Klub Lávka and La Fabrique lean towards cheesy, poptastic fun, while slightly more discerning club nights and live gigs take place at Wenceslas Square's Duplex or Dlouha's Roxy. Regular nightclubs – as opposed to those that hold special gigs and international DJ nights – rarely charge entrance fees, and if they do they are often minimal. In general, drinks are more expensive in clubs than in bars and pubs, but only slightly so, and some still offer booze at surprisingly reasonable prices.

The cooler clubs lie outside the city centre. If you're planning on donning designer togs and checking out some cutting-edge sounds, just book a taxi (and do book, since street taxis are notorious for stinging tourists) and head to Radost FX or Mecca. If you're gagging for more when the lights flick on, there are after-hours clubs such as Le Clan and Studio 54 that will see you through to the daylight hours.

Czech jazz, although no longer at the cutting edge of the European scene, has a history that stretches back to the end of World War II. Consequently there is a host of jazz clubs dotted around the city that put on nightly programmes. Some, such as Ungelt and U Staré Pani, put on local jazz and blues bands, while others, such as Reduta, cater for the avant-garde 'roll-neck' crowd. AghaRTA seems to be the only current spot to catch top-class international acts. Since most of these clubs are bona fide jazz cellars, the atmosphere is usually great, no matter what the band or night. There is generally an entrance fee that ranges from about 200 to 300kc.

A visit to a casino can make or break a great weekend. You might win enough money to pay the hotel bill; you might also end up losing the taxi fare to the airport the next day. If you do decide to try your luck, you can be assured that Prague's casinos, while not as opulent as elsewhere in the world, are usually great fun and provide interesting people-watching opportunities.

Minimum bets are similar to England, while the maximum is considerably less, whether you're playing in crowns or dollars. Prague is rapidly becoming a gambling junket destination, with gamblers from Greece, Turkey and the Middle East filling the casinos for days at a time. While most casinos don't charge for entry, they will require you to have a passport, even if you are not betting. Soft drinks are invariably free to all; free beer and wine is strictly for the players; and food is free if you become a high-roller. There are no restrictions on licensing and you are allowed to drink at the tables.

Prague has also gained legendary status for its array of adult entertainment. From computerized brothels with space age rooms, such as K5 (above) to run-of-the-mill lap dancing clubs (Goldfingers). More committed hedonists can find information at the end of this section.

Akropolis, Kubelíkova 27, Žižkov

Tel: 296 330 911 www.palacakropolis.cz
Open: daily, 4pm–4am

Akropolis is one of Prague's legendary venues. Rough, ready and very popular with young Czechs, it's set in a sprawling complex that houses (at street level) a canteen-style restaurant serving decent food and a concert venue that promotes both local bands and international stars. If you voyage below ground-floor level you'll find a basement club where DJs spin a variety of styles, from funk and hip-hop to techno and trance. The downstairs club is

the primary space for weekends, and boasts two different areas: a smaller bar that tends to play harder beats or hip-hop, and a slightly larger area that favours a more funk/reggae sound. While most Prague drinking venues are smoky, Akropolis' smoke has a slightly sweeter scent, coming principally from the city's spliffnoscenti. Shabby around the edges it may be, but the drinks are cheap, the tunes are good and it's usually free to get in.

Le Clan, Balbínova 23, Vinohrady

Tel: 222 25 12 26 www.leclan.cz
Open: midnight–7am Fri–Sat

The lights have come on but you still want to dance. It's 3am but everyone else is heading home. Enter Le Clan, Vinohrady's latest after-hours club. This place doesn't even get started before 3am and is happy to play host to the city's nocturnal wanderers – as long as they look the part. Finding Le Clan is a mission in itself since there is no sign for the club outside and it's situated beneath a residential block, but once you have found it (just scan the area for any likely clubbers and ask), the night begins anew as Le Clan's dedicated

DJs provide rhythmic fuel until the early hours. This trendy space offers comfortable couches and opium-den chic for when you need to get your feet off the floor. Le Clan definitely draws the city's most fabulous freaks, and is also popular with a discerning international audience. Entrance at weekends is free until 2am, after which you'll have to dish out a 100kc cover charge.

Duplex, Václavské náměstí 21, Nové Město
Tel: 257 535 050 www.duplexduplex.cz
Open: daily, 11pm–3am (5am Fri–Sat)

Located on the sixth floor of a building in the centre of Wenceslas Square, this rooftop club-bar and restaurant enjoys fantastic views of Prague and its majestic Castle lit up at night. The entranceway off the street is fairly anony-

mous, but a lift swiftly transports you up to a funkier lobby. The club itself looks like a Playboy video, with industrial walkways and cages hanging over the dance-floor. Seats in the booths around the side face towards huge windows, offering views over the hustle-bustle of the square below.

Duplex attracts a strange mix of players: the high entrance fee and inflated drinks prices are prohibitive to many locals, so business people and tourists take their place. The regular DJs play a mix of chart and house music, while international DJs drop in from time to time to raise the tempo. Staff add to the eye candy, which is just as well, since they aren't there for their speed or friendliness.

La Fabrique, Uhelný trh 2, Staré Město
Tel: 224 233 137 www.lafabrique.cz
Open: daily, 11am–3am

Just outside the main tourist area, this is yet another example of the cheesier end of Prague's clubbing scene. Located on a small, pretty square just along from the KU Café (Drink) and Café Café (Snack), La Fabrique invites you to descend into the bowels of the city, whereupon you will find, on the first floor, a thriving bar and restaurant area. One more level down, you'll hit

a bar and dance-floor, which seems to be nearly always packed with ex-pats, young Czech secretaries and students in search of one another. There's usually a local house or R'n'B jock presenting a mix of dance and pop tunes. If the heat starts to go to your head, clamber back upstairs where it's more relaxed – and there's a quicker bar service. Raucous La Fabrique is not for the faint-hearted, but if you want a fun night out and an opportunity to meet some of the locals, then this could be the best place.

Karlovy Lázně, Novotného Lávka, Staré Mesto
Tel: 222 220 502 www.karlovylazne.cz
Open: daily, 9pm–5am

Located on a promontory into the Vltava, Karlovy Lázně is reckoned to be the largest club in Central Europe. If that idea fills you full of fear, perhaps it should. The reality is worse: five floors packed to the rafters with young, sweaty, style-conscious types (mostly American college kids), downing cheap

drinks and getting busy to a range of sounds from techno to rock and pop (there's a different genre on each floor). It may well be a vision of hell for some; for others, it presents a wonderful opportunity to throw themselves into a non-judgemental crowd and party the night away.

Klub Lávka, Novotného Lávka 1, Staré Město
Tel: 222 222 156 www.lavka.cz
Open: daily, 10pm–4am

Lávka sits beside Karlovy Lázně on the very edge of the riverbank, giving the impression that they are connected; they're not. Lávka has fantastic views up towards the Castle and over Charles Bridge, and where its brash neighbour caters for the masses, Lávka entertains a slightly more discriminating crowd. Don't get too dolled up to play, however, since we're not talking super-hip here. In fact the interior is extremely kitsch, as is the music (mostly chart hits and old faves), but the crowd are older and wiser than at Karlovy Lázně and there is always the fantastic terrace to escape to if things don't work out to your liking. You'll generally be sharing that view, as well as

most of the dark corners, with other tourists – the only Czechs you'll find in here will probably expect their drinks, entry and everything else paid for.

Lucerna Music Bar, Vodičkova 36, Nové Město
Tel; 224 217 108 www.musicbar.cz
Open: daily, 8pm–3am

One of the best live venues in the city centre, Lucerna is housed in an old theatre that exudes a simple, basic charm. Spread over two floors, at the entrance to a large shopping arcade on a street leading from Wenceslas Square, this venue plays host to regular, decent bands (home-grown and international), and there are also lively 1980s and '90s parties at weekends. It's cheap and cheerful, so expect basic tables, school chairs and plastic beer mugs – the young Czech market it is geared to certainly don't seem to

mind. There are bars on both floors with a stage dominating the ground level, while upstairs the atmosphere is a little more relaxed. This is a great choice if an interesting band is playing, or if you simply want to enjoy a frugal night out in the centre of town.

Mecca, U průhonu 3, Holešovice

Tel: 283 870 522 www.mecca.cz
Open: 11am–10pm Mon–Thurs; noon–6am Fri–Sat

Prague clubs don't get much cooler than this: imagine the rumbling bass of cutting-edge dance tunes and ice-blonde über-babes elegantly ignoring bumbling tourists, and you're almost there. It's expensive by Prague standards, but judging by the amount of designer clothing and luxury accessories on display, the clientele probably don't even notice. Naturally the design is chic and individual, with a great lighting system, sleek modern furnishings and large, comfortable chairs. The bar staff wouldn't look out of place in a Vogue

shoot, the tunes are masterminded by knowing domestic and international DJs, and the emphasis is just as much on posing and people-watching as it is on dancing. Open during the day as a café and restaurant, this is also a good place to unwind and glow after a hard night's exertion. It does involve a short taxi ride, but serious clubbers will be glad they made the trip.

Radost FX, Bělehradská 120, Vinohrady

Tel: 224 254 776 www.radostfx.cz
Open: 10pm–5am. Closed Mondays and Tuesdays.

The best known of the city's clubbing spots, Radost FX was once included in the Ministry of Sound's Top 20 Best Clubs in the World list – and it still hasn't lost its edge. Radost remains the epitome of cool on the Prague scene, frequented by ex-pats, celebrities and 'proper' clubbers alike, who come here to check out the international DJs and some of the best local jocks the city has to offer. The main club is made up of a large, futuristic bar, a retro-looking chill-out room with large sofas and comfortable chairs, and a small but perfectly formed dance-floor with balconies conveniently placed above to look down on the party below. Weekends are the best time to come here, but it also stages established nights throughout the week. If you get a little peckish the vegetarian café upstairs (see Snack) serves fantastic food into the early hours.

Roxy, Dlouhá 33, Josefov
Tel: 224 826 296 www.roxy.cz
Open: daily, 10pm–4am

A venerable Prague mainstay, the Roxy has been bringing bands and DJs of international acclaim to the city for many years. A short stroll from Old Town Square, the venue boasts a prime location, and although its huge concrete bunker interior isn't radical or cutting edge, the crowds love it for what it is and what it represents: a no-frills venue with an emphasis on very good music. Expect basic benches and school assembly chairs rather than zebra-skin sofas, and plastic beakers as opposed to Martini glasses; also expect musical styles that range from house to ska to rock. The drinks are cheap and weed-smoke fills the air. It's sometimes frenetic, other times

chilled; and you'll do well to find out what's on beforehand unless you're up for a bit of a surprise.

Solidní Nejistota, Pštrossova 21, Nové Město
Tel: 224 933 086   www.solidninejistota.cz
Open: daily, 7pm–6am

Something of an 'in' spot for the local 20- and early 30-something crowd, Solidni Nejistota is popular also with B-list actors, models and sports stars who hang out in this intriguing club/jazz bar. The room is dominated by a

large, central bar, but don't expect getting drinks to be a swift experience; you can spend a fair time trying to be noticed, and then served. The venue is often packed with beautiful women who happily drink themselves into near oblivion, then hit the handkerchief-sized dance-floor in dinky outfits to groove to cheesy pop. However, the meat market doesn't end here, as Solidni also serves up a late-night steak or two – the grill bar stays open 'til 4am. Be slightly careful, since some of these ladies are looking for a little cash incentive to leave with you.

Studio 54, Hybernská 38, Nové Město

Tel: n/a   www.studio54.cz
Open: 5am–3pm Sat

Another of Prague's infamous after-hours clubs, Studio 54 isn't as sexy as Le Clan, but it is popular. This venue draws a friendly, up-for-it crowd who come here for the party atmosphere and the consistently decent beats laid

down by some of the city's best DJs. The music policy ranges from big, fast electronic sounds to sensual, deep house. As the night outside makes its inexorable move towards daylight, a varied mix of locals and foreigners, club-heads and workers flow through the doors and into the club's welcoming darkness. By the time it gets to 7 or 8 in the morning, the venue is not necessarily going to appeal to the faint-hearted: only dedicated hedonists need apply.

Zero, Dusní 8, Josefov

Tel: 739 096 779 www.myspace.com/zeroprague
Open: daily, 10pm–4am (6am Fri–Sat)

Conveniently situated between a wealth of restaurants, traditional pubs and swanky cocktail bars north of Old Town, Zero is the place you might want to look in on if you're in the mood for some decent electronic sounds. The

space isn't huge but Zero has already made a name among local hipsters with its erudite music policy and cute, futuristic interior. Through the week the venue is pretty laid back, with the odd DJ or laptop don throwing out tunes. Come the weekend, however, when doors are open until 6am, Zero can get its swerve on. With 120 cocktails to choose from, Pilsner Urquell on tap and a heavy mix of breaks, electro, house and drum & bass on offer, there's just no telling what kind of shenanigans might go down.

JAZZ CLUBS

AghaRTA Jazz Centrum, Železná 16, Staré Město
Tel: 222 211 275 www.agharta.cz
Open: daily, 6pm–12.30am

Located close to Old Town Square, AghaRTA is one of the more considered and well-placed jazz spots in the city. Opened by the owners of the well-known ARTA record label, the club was born the day after Miles Davis died (28 September 1991), and is

named after one of his albums. The wonderful exposed brickwork cellar hosts the most varied and impressive line-up in the city, rotating local jazz, fusion, blues, modern jazz and soul bands with the odd international guest. The bar serves great coffee and carries on the Davis tributes with drinks titled 'Bitches' Brew' and 'Blue In Green' – there is even a dedicated record shop on site. AghaRTA have also been running a high-profile annual jazz festival since 1992 that's still going strong. Concerts start at 9pm; check the website for details of all the events.

U Malého Glena, Karmelitská 23, Malá Strana
Tel: 257 531 717 www.malyglen.cz
Open: daily, 10am–2am

From the outside this looks like a typical Czech/Irish pub advertising live gigs by dodgy tribute bands. Fortunately, that's not the case. The club downstairs is a live music lounge that promotes young Czech jazz at its finest, bringing in established musicians as well as a great deal of up-and-coming talent. The sound in the tiny vaulted cellar is intense, and the audience so close to the musicians that a skilled spectator could reach out and play a solo on one of the instruments without moving from their seat. The room

only holds 20 or so bodies and can get hot and sweaty pretty quickly. Drinks are cheap and the crowd (a mix of locals and tourists) tends to be passionate. Definitely worth a visit, although perhaps the Sunday night free-for-all is best avoided.

Reduta, Národní 20, Staré Město

Tel: 224 912 246 www.redutajazzclub.cz
Open: daily, 9pm–midnight

This traditional jazz club first opened in 1958, but was made famous by Bill Clinton, who played his saxophone here – presumably without inhaling – alongside President Havel. A large, old-fashioned and slightly stuffy room, the

space boasts a series of angular sofas, black-and-white prints of jazz legends on the walls and a serious line-up of modern, classic and fusion jazz bands. Since it's not in a cellar and the bar is hidden away in a side room, the atmosphere is slightly more formal than elsewhere, heightening the idea that it's a venue for aficionados only. However, this is emphatically not the case, and even a beginner can enjoy sitting back and listening to a riff here. The room thaws out when the bands get going, and this is still a great place to combine quality music with a couple of quiet drinks.

U Staré Pani, Michalská 9, Staré Město

Tel: 603 551 680 www.jazzlounge.cz
Open: daily, 7pm–2am

Once upon a time, 'At the Old Woman's' was a brothel. Since 2002, however, the space has housed this jazz club – one of the only such establishments where you can enjoy a reasonable meal with your music. Although it's located in a cellar (entrance is via the lobby of the U Staré Pani hotel), the venue is far from dingy – it's a spacious, well-organized and very orange place, populated with rows of tables and chairs, and with quite a flash bar at

the back. The food menu stretches to some original and exotic options (including Thai soups, grilled goat and burritos), while the musical carte is mostly made up of consummate Czech musicians who play modern jazz, Latin, blues and even funk and swing, with one evening per month set aside for unknown, amateur bands.

Ungelt Jazz & Blues Club, Týn 2 (entrance on Týnská ulička), Staré Město

Tel: 224 895 748 www.jazzblues.cz
Open: daily, 8pm–midnight

One of the best known and mainstreamed of the city's jazz bars, Ungelt is a small, underground cellar with an enviable location just behind the stunning Tyn Church (Old Town Square). After passing through a slightly confusing and brightly lit restaurant you descend some steps into the venue proper,

which is split into two areas: a bar and a live performance space. Both are intimate, to say the least. Bands tend to be high-profile and home-grown rather than internationally famous, but the quality of musicianship is generally high. You can choose to hang out at the bar and listen to the show for free (beers and mixers are on offer, rather than cocktails), or pay to sit in the small concert room (it used to be a coal cellar) and absorb the heavenly barrage of minor fifths at close range. Ungelt has broad appeal, and you'll probably be enjoying the sounds among a varied crowd consisting of tourists, young aficionados, families and older folk.

CASINOS

Ambassador Casino, Václavské náměstí 5, Nové Město
Tel: 224 193 681
Open: 24 hours daily

Located on the top floor of the Ambassador Hotel on Wenceslas Square, this casino's overriding virtue is its central location. The complex includes a large hotel and a 'top class' lap-dancing bar, should you feel like spending your hard-earned gambling winnings immediately. The casino itself is modern and clean, with a mixture of slot machines and gaming tables. There are four blackjack and roulette tables as well as a poker table; bets start at 25kc for roulette and 100kc for blackjack. Although it's not entirely obvious, soft drinks and beer are free for players; everything else you have to pay for. The 24-hour opening means that even after everything else is closed you can still fritter away the last of your money here. The Ambassador tends to be full of tourists, and attracts a pre- and post-lap-dancing stag crowd from downstairs.

Casino Palace Savarin, Na Příkopě 10, Staré Město
Tel: 224 221 636
Open: daily, 1pm–4am

A grand, old-fashioned room complete with coruscating chandeliers, Savarin is an extremely friendly, courteous and professional place. The beautiful old baroque building dates back to the mid-18th century, and its impressive entrance from the street accurately hints at the sophistication found inside. The stuccoed and columned interior is packed full of glamour — a dashing 007 wouldn't be out of place here. The casino has five blackjack and six roulette tables, a pontoon and a poker table, and bets range from 20kc to 30,000kc. A separate room for high rollers provides free food and drink, while mere mortals receive free soft drinks, wine and beer while they are playing (there is a small restaurant that serves good meals). This venue is a favourite of the ex-pat community and, although central, it tends to be fairly free of tourists or gambling junkets from abroad. Savarin is doubtlessly the most sophisticated casino in the city.

ADULT ENTERTAINMENT

Atlas, Ve Smečkách 31, Nové Město
Tel: 296 224 260 www.atlas-cabaret.cz
Open: daily, 7pm–7am

A largish 'nightclub' just off Wenceslas Square, Atlas is one of the longer-running adult clubs in town. An impressively large array of girls, mostly stunning, drape themselves across the red leather chairs or sashay around the dancing pole, although these same beauties can be somewhat aggressive on the 'buy-me-a-drink' (or 'buy me') front. You will be given a drinks card on entry — do not lose it or you will be charged an extortionate amount to leave the place. If you don't feel the need to partake, be aware that there are also live strippers on stage as well as the occasional live sex show.

Big Sister, Nádražní 46, Smíchov
Tel: 257 310 043 www.bigsister.net
Open: daily, 6pm–3am

Big Sister boasts girls, a restaurant, a bar, a place to watch porn and rooms to have sex in. Oh, and around two dozen webcams that film everything inside and beam it out live to the internet via the Big Sister website. This brothel/porn film-set could possibly be the most innovative idea since the invention of the brothel itself, appealing to voyeurs (who must of course pay for access to the online webcams) and exhibitionists alike. After paying a minimal entrance fee (500kc), the staff will produce a detailed contract (don't forget your ID – a passport is recommended), which gives them the legal right to film all activities in the club and display the contents on their pay site. In exchange you get a girl, a room and an hour's action free of charge. The girls aren't as gorgeous or numerous as at K5, but there are certainly enough to provide a decent choice. If performing live sex shows isn't your thing, there is a more discreet strip club downstairs (no cameras) where you can watch girls on poles and/or hire a private room for cheaper rates than elsewhere.

Darling Cabaret, Ve Smečkách 32a, Nové Město
Tel. 608 666 949 www.kabaret.cz
Open: daily, 12pm–5am

Located almost directly opposite Atlas Cabaret, Darling is one of the larger and more popular adult clubs in town. The venue boasts no fewer than four bars, up to 150 women during the weekend, and 20 themed rooms for making the house shake. The large main space has a central stage, where girls dance around poles and perform strips and lesbian acts, while there are also smaller rooms available that provide a little more intimacy. The security is tight, the girls are generally top class, and you can even arrange to turn up in a free limo (subject to availability; call 732 250 555).

Goldfingers, Václavské náměstí 5, Nové Město
Tel: 224 193 856
Open: daily, 9pm–4am

Goldfingers is the smartest and best-groomed strip-club in town, home to elegant, leggy supermodels. Dances cost 1,000kc, while a more private dance (touching allowed) costs 1,500kc. This is the full extent of the funny business – extra-curricular activities are strictly not on the menu. As the name might suggest, playing here is expensive, and drinks and dances are pricey in comparison with other strip joints or bars. At the entrance a cover of 450kc is charged, and for this you get a professional, 'not in your face' experience. As such, Goldfingers can offer a good, safe introduction to the more sophisticated side of Prague porn.

K5, Korunní 5, Nové Město

Tel: 224 250 505   www.k5relax.com

Open: daily, 4pm—4am

K5 is the undisputed king of Prague's sex scene: clean, stylish and run with the kind of professionalism you'd expect from a five-star hotel. The building is furnished with a club, bar/restaurant, a relaxation area featuring a sauna, steam room and professional massage equipment and, of course, 15 individually themed rooms in which to enjoy yourself and your new friend. On arrival you can take a seat in the downstairs bar or upstairs in the main club. Refreshingly, the girls are not allowed to approach you in K5; you must choose them before they sit down and talk to you (this means that, happily, you don't get hassled for drinks as soon as you walk in). Aiding you in your search for Ms Right (For The Night) are the enthusiastic staff as well as slide-out computer terminals under the tables, which give you all the vital, which information you need. The 500kc entrance fee can be claimed back if you choose a girl right away, or you can simply relax hassle-free, enjoying a cold drink, the entertainment of a skilful pole dance and the civilized gentleman's club ambience.

Club Nights & Telephone Numbers

Hg2 Prague

culture...

Prague is, hands down, one of the most beautiful cities in the whole of Europe – a truly breathtaking synthesis of architectural grandeur, riveting history and generous amounts of culture, past and present.

Unlike Paris or Rome, there isn't a world-famous cultural museum or gallery for sightseers to gravitate to – there's no Louvre, or Vatican; instead, Praha's charms often lie not in any obvious location but in the sheen of the tiny cobbled streets, the discreet architectural surprises, and the mysterious and magical ambience that the city weaves around you.

Charles Bridge and Old Town Square are the obvious tourist draws, but most of the churches, buildings and streets around the centre and Malá Strana are also worth exploring, since they tell stories about the city and its people that date back centuries.

Prague is world-renowned for its arts and culture – several musical genres have their roots here, and it has a strong tradition of theatre and dance. The city boasts three beautiful opera houses, which stage magnificent perform-

ances of classic operas. Tickets are incredibly cheap compared with London, and you are seated closer to the action. We highly recommend going to a performance – often held on

a Saturday afternoon – and since repertoires mainly consist of old favourites, it could prove a good introduction to opera (subtitles are often provided in English).

Most of the plays are in Czech, but some have subtitles, and in other theatres you may be able to listen to an English translation on headphones.
Black light theatre is another particular Czech favourite. This involves a stage set in near-total darkness, luminous paint/suits and ultraviolet lights, creating a space in  which shapes appear to float weightlessly in front of the audience. Other forms of theatrical entertainment include a marionette version of *Don Giovanni*, which, surprisingly enough, goes down well even with opera lovers.

Every night the medley of concerts for which Prague is renowned are performed across the city, often in stunning surroundings. The concert venues are either purpose-built, such as the Dvorak and Smetana concert halls, or churches, most of which are architectural gems. The standard of music is high, with pieces representing all the major composers but with an obvious preference for the Czech greats. It's a wonderfully civilized way to spend an afternoon and evening. And what could be more memorable than listening to a string quartet in a candlelit baroque church?

Charles Bridge (Karluv Most), Staré Město

Construction on the bridge began in 1357 but was only finished at the beginning of the 15th century. Immediately identifiable by its dramatic array of 17th-century baroque statues (depicting various saints), and by its smart-looking tower bridges at both ends, the bridge has become one of Prague's most iconic symbols – and it shows. By day it's packed with tourists flowing

in both directions, periodically pausing to admire the views, have their caricature sketched, watch a jazz band or buy a trinket. The only time you can get it to yourself (more or less) is early in the morning or late at night, and even then you still might have to share your experience with the remnants of rowdy groups of foreigners out on the town. Budding numerologists and ardent palindromists may be interested in the digits carved into the Old Town Bridge Tower – '135797531'. They represent the precise moment – 5.31am on 9 July, 1357 – when Charles IV laid the foundation stone for the bridge, as advised by his royal court of astrologers and number-crunchers.

Franz Kafka Museum, Hergetova Cihelná, Cihelná 2b, Malá Strana

Tel: 221 451 333 www.kafkamuseum.cz
Open: daily, 10am–6pm   Admission: 120kc

Despite the colossal reputation of Prague's most famous literary son, this is one of the city's newer museums, set up around the same time as the first Kafka statue was erected on Dusní street (2004). Better late than never, of course, and what the Museum has lost in belatedness it makes up for with a fantastically comprehensive analysis of Kafka's life, insights into his major works, his social life and relationships, plus plenty of original letters, manu-

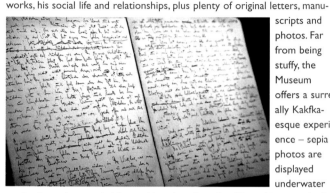

scripts and photos. Far from being stuffy, the Museum offers a surreally Kakfkaesque experience – sepia photos are displayed underwater on the floor, claustrophobic corridors host looming filing cabinets, and ethereal images are projected onto fragile textiles and into mirrored spaces. All the way through, a sinister soundtrack of ringing phones, squawking crows and mysterious bells provides a suitably paranoid atmosphere. A café and bookstore are located directly opposite for those thirsty for a drink/inspiration.

House of the Black Madonna, Celetná 34, Staré Město
Tel: 222 220 218 www.cmvu.cz
Open: 10am–6pm. Closed Mondays.   Admission: 50kc

Otherwise known as the Czech Museum of Fine Arts, the House of the Black Madonna was designed by renowned Czech architect Josef Gocar, who was commissioned to build a department store and ended up creating one of the city's finest examples of architectural Cubism. In 1994 the building's metamorphosis from store to museum was made with the launch of its first permanent exhibition. It was then closed down in 2002, reopening again in 2003. Today the main attractions – apart from the building itself – can be found on the second, third and fourth floors, which house some of the best examples of the country's vibrant Cubist scene. Created by young Czech artists mainly between 1911 and 1919, paintings, drawings, sculptures and furniture by the likes of Gocar, Pavel Janak, Vlastislav Hofman and Josef

Chochol are on display here. There's also an erudite bookstore on the ground floor and the beautifully reconstructed Grand Café Orient up above.

Kampa Museum, U Sovových Mlýnů 2, Malá Strana
Tel: 257 286 147 www.museumkampa.cz
Open: daily, 10am–6pm

The Kampa Museum is situated on the river bank overlooking the Old Town, the Charles Bridge and the National Theatre. Housed in an old mill that dates back to the 14th century, the Museum opened in 2003, a year later than planned because of the 2002 floods. The renovation has created a wonderfully contemporary space in which the best of Czech modern art is displayed. Its permanent collection includes works by František Kupka and Otto Gutfreund as well as prominent Central European artists, and there are regular temporary exhibitions. Apart from the beautiful architecture and thought-

provoking art, the Kampa Museum offers a delicious and tempting café, Sovovy Mlyny, where you can reflect on the meaning of it all while casually demolishing a cream cake.

Mucha Museum, Panská 7, Nové Město

Tel: 221 451 333
Open: daily, 10am–6pm

The Czech Republic's favourite artist-son, Alphonse Mucha (1860–1939) was one of the most internationally celebrated artists of the Art Nouveau period. Among his most famous posters were those he designed for the great fin-de-siècle actress, Sarah Bernhardt. Mucha moved to Paris towards the

end of the 19th century, where he spent time on individual commissions, designing advertising posters and shop façades. The Mucha Museum, a celebration of his art and life, is housed in the lavish Kaunicky Palace; the gallery space is located on the ground floor. Works are hung under the low-vaulted ceiling, with simple wooden floors and plain white walls showing off his colourful pieces to full effect. This is one of the most popular museums in town, and well worth a visit for a better understanding of the subtler undercurrents of the Art Nouveau movement.

Old Town Square (Staroméstské námestí), Staré Město

Old Town Square is Prague's awe-inspiring focal point. Looking like a beautiful film set, bordered by elegant façades representing a bewildering mixture

of architectural periods, it exudes an eternal, fairy-tale quality, enhanced by a run of terrific buildings: the Gothic Tyn church, the unique Astronomical Clock, the 14th-century Old Town Hall, and the baroque St Nicholas Church. Tourists throng the square day and night, congregating around the clock to photograph, document and experience its incredibly short, and somewhat pitiful, hourly rigmarole. Take the time to climb to the top of the Old Town Hall tower (next to the clock) for a panoramic vista across the city.

Prague Castle (Pražský Hrad), Hradčany

Prague Castle, the largest medieval castle in the world, can be seen rising dramatically over the district of Malá Strana, imposing itself on the city sky-

line at all hours of the day and night. It's a fairly steep walk to the top, but worth it, of course, not only for its history and architecture but also for the peerless views. Work started on the Castle as far back as the 9th century, with the original complex gradually expanding into the veritable mini-town it is now. The focal point is St Vitus's Cathedral, but the romanesque basilica of St George, the monastery, various palaces, art galleries and defence towers also demand your attention. History-lovers will want to spend at least an afternoon here, if not a whole day exploring the grounds; thankfully there are plenty of cafés around too.

Royal Way, Staré Město/Hradčany

The Royal Way is the path that runs from Náměstí Republiky to Old Town Square and up to the castle, crossing the Charles Bridge on the way. It winds through the narrow cobbled streets of the Old Town towards the river, then up the hill on the other side, past the grand St Nicholas Church to the entrance to the castle. The streets are lined with shops packed to the

gunnels with Prague Drinking Team T-shirts, miniature model houses, cheap glassware and millions more relatively worthless souvenirs. Yet not even this trail of tack (nor the ubiquitous tour groups) detracts from the regal beauty of the route, blessed as it is with supreme examples of medieval and baroque architecture. If you want to avoid the hordes and the hawkers, this journey is best enjoyed late at night or early in the morning.

CONCERTS

Klementinum, Karlova, Staré Město
Tel: 221 663 200

The Chapel of Mirrors in this church, located in the centre of the Old Town, arguably boasts the best church acoustics in Prague. The intimate space holds no more than 100 people, who sit surrounded by fantastic gold baroque ornamentation and a plethora of mirrors that reflect the candle-light. The music is eclectic, ranging from chamber music to Dvorak.

Prague Castle, Hradčany
Tel: 224 373 368   www.hrad.cz

Chorales and symphonies are sometimes held in the neo-Gothic splendour of St Vitus' Cathedral or the Spanish Hall. If you can find tickets to an event here, snap them up – particularly if they are for the one-off spectaculars (see the website for advance notices and bookings).

Rudolfinium, Náměstí Jana Palacha, Josefov
Tel: 224 893 352   www.czechphilharmonic.cz

An immense neo-Renaissance building on the bank of the Vltava, the Rudolfinium is the official home of the Czech Philharmonic, its roof adorned with statues of famous composers. When the Germans rolled into Prague in 1938, they were aware that one of these represented Mendelssohn, who was Jewish. Unable to discover from the records which this was, they decid-ed to look for the one with the biggest nose and tear it down. It is rather satisfying to learn that the statue they actually destroyed turned out to be of Wagner, the famous German composer. The CPO perform in the main Dvořák Hall, which seats 1,200, while the smaller Little Hall is more suited to chamber music. Restored comprehensively in the 1990s, it also contains a rather splendid café.

St Nicholas Church, Staroméstské Náměstí, Staré Město

Located in a corner of Old Town Square, this gorgeous baroque church has nightly recitals that normally draw in crowds of tourists. Completed in 1737, the splendid interior combines ornate architecture and stucco with acoustics that are better suited to a booming organ than a haunting violin.

Smetana Hall, Náměstí Republiky 5, Staré Město
www.obecnidum.cz

Housed in the Municipal House, the Smetana Hall occupies the central section of the building and is home to the Prague Symphony Orchestra. There are three other smaller halls here, but the Smetana can hold almost 1,100 people (meaning you will probably be able to find a spare seat). Keep an eye open for the people in costume outside, who sell tickets and are a good source of information about what's on and when. The website has the best information about the larger upcoming concerts, however, especially those of the PSO.

OPERA

Národní Divadlo, Národní 2, Staré Město
Tel: 224 913 437 www.narodni-divadlo.cz

The National Theatre, opened in 1881, is located on the river bank and forms part of the fantastic frontage that symbolizes the city. Its gold roof catches the sun, particularly in the evening, and can be seen from miles around. Internally it is similar to the Estates Theatre, with a sumptuous red and gold interior spread over four levels. Tickets can be purchased from the box office around the corner from the theatre or on the evening of the performance from the foyer, as well as online. However, for the best deals and most accurate information on the seats available, head straight to the box office – performances often sell out, so for higher-end tickets, a little research may be needed. The programme is a mixed rotation of opera, ballet and theatre, which requires intense daily set changes.

Státní opera Praha, Wilsonova 4, Nové Město
Tel: 224 227 693 www.opera.cz

The State Opera House is to be found at the top end of Wenceslas Square, close to the National Museum. Internally similar to the other opera houses of Prague, it has lavish gold and red furnishings decorated with ornate baroque swirls. Operas are staged every day, the majority Italian, with Verdi a firm favourite. Occasionally works by German and Russian composers add a little variety to the bill. While the House itself is a wee walk from the centre, the experience is well worth the journey, and can be combined with a trip to the Zahrada v Opeře, one of Prague's finest restaurants (found in the same complex). The box office is on the left, and tickets are available from the foyer as well on the evening of the performance.

Stavovské divadlo, Ovocný třída 6, Staré Město
Tel: 224 215 001 www.opera.cz

The Estates Theatre is most famous for hosting the world première of Mozart's *Don Giovanni*, conducted by the man himself. Its elegant façade forms the backdrop to Rytířská street, with its classical columns and ornate pediments. Inside, the blue and gold interior is stunning and relatively small, so the performances seem far more intimate than those in other venues of the same stature. Events alternate between theatre and opera, the latter inevitably featuring Mozart. Tickets can be bought at the entrance for forthcoming performances or for that night, as well as from the National Theatre box office on Národní. If you can, book your tickets before you travel to Prague; it's well worth getting a box.

Concert Schedule

shop...

The question that will probably greet you when you enter a shop in Prague is '*Máte přání?*' meaning both 'Can I help you?' and 'What is your wish?' Whereas before the Velvet Revolution the pickings for wishes were limited, the city now offers shopping districts rivalling those of other large European capitals. Whether you're searching for crystal, garnets or the latest couture, you can now find them on the magic streets of Prague, or in the slightly more dull but convenient shopping arcades.

Prague is internationally renowned for its glassware, and as with other traditional products, you can find glass and crystal that ranges in quality from pieces of art to cheap tack. Much of the glass is very ornate (perhaps too much for some people's sensibilities), but if you want to buy an engraved piece, splurge a bit more for the heavier glass and packaging so that it lasts beyond the check-in point. There are bargains to be had if you know what you're looking for – particularly in the city's galleries and antique shops.

There are various other products that are fairly ubiquitous around town: marionettes and dolls are for sale in many of the tourist shops, but these toys are substantially scarier than many children – or adults, come to that – can actually stomach. Wooden toys are also to be found in abundance, and the market at

Havelska is particularly good for cheap toys that can keep small children amused for a while. Garnets are mined down the road in Teplice and are used in jewellery sold in almost every jeweller's shop in Prague. The deep red stones are very attractive, and said to bring luck to those who wear them, but are often set in over-elaborate surrounds and displayed in cases that often seem to light up entire streets.

Shopping in Prague has become far more cosmopolitan in recent years, with many of the top international fashion houses now making their presence felt in

the city. British high-street stores such as Tesco, offering all the necessary basics, have gained a foothold in the market, along with similar competition from the rest of Europe. You can find almost everything you need in the city, so leaving a cosmetics case or a suit at home becomes more of an excuse to go shopping than a nuisance.

As the demand for quality shopping in the city grows, stores are spilling out of centres and arcades into side streets and quaint alleyways, so don't be afraid to explore the areas around the main avenues to find interesting boutiques. Key finds for souvenirs can be routed out in the markets of the city, particularly in the weeks leading up to Christmas. Most shops accept credit cards, but finding a shop assistant who speaks English can be difficult. If you don't want to carry your purchases around with you, many of the high-end shops will send your items to your hotel, leaving you unburdened to roam the streets of the city for as long as you desire.

NOVE MĚSTO – THE NEW TOWN

Jungmannova Náměstí, Nové Město

Lurking behind Wenceslas Square, this little plaza works just as well as a convenient walkway as it does a small shopping parade.

Adidas a wide range of products, including footwear, for men and women
Boss the best of this contemporary designer fashion is available here, as well as in several other stores throughout the city
Lancôme a fully stocked, well-set-out store carrying this French line
Marc Aurel/Bianca boutique fashions for women
Terranova Italian high-street fashion for men and women spread over two floors

Koruna Palace, Václavské Náměstí, Nové Město
www.koruna-palace.cz

An airy Art Nouveau shopping centre on a corner of Wenceslas Square, Koruna has a pizzeria, gelato eatery and a diverse selection of international shops.

Accessorize a chain store by the British designers of Monsoon
Anima Tua eclectic women's wear from a range of individual designers
Bontonland a giant Czech music store carrying CDs, DVDs and games
Kenvelo a sporty-yet-stylish Czech clothing collection offering a large selection for men, women and children
Oilily incredibly sweet and funky children's clothing and accessory line from Holland
Swatch a complete selection of the Swiss watch company's range of practical and designer time-pieces and jewellery

Lucerna Passage, Vodickova, Nové Město
www.lucerna.cz/pasaz.php

With palace halls that sometimes host fashion shows but normally only contain small collections of tourists photographing the large upside-down horse (hanging from the ceiling), Lucerna offers a daily passage to history. The arcade contains shops that stock photography equipment, musical instruments, ceramics and handbags. Whether you're looking for an antique camera, or just wanting to step off the street for a quick wander through to a café or restaurant, the Lucerna Passage is worth a fast detour.

Myslbek, Na Příkopě, Nové Město
www.myslbek.com

A large mall off this busy shopping street houses an ample selection of international stores. The centre feels modern and open – as if you could be shopping in any mall around the world, although a large number of the bigger stores are British chains.

Bibelot a small shop offering high-end pens and accessories. With a selection of names including Montblanc, it's the perfect location to pick up a stylish business gift.

Delmas premium-quality leather products, specializing in bags and briefcases but still carrying accessory lines and a selection of Czech products

Gant the all-American store that offers a clean-cut and preppy look

GigaSport a huge sporting store, carrying apparel and equipment

H&M affordable modern British apparel for men, women and children

Mothercare an outlet for the British chain, selling a range of baby clothes and accessories

Next a large British 'value for style' chain shop, with fashions for men and women

Slovansky Dům, Na Příkopě, Nové Město
www.slovanskydum.cz

Ostensibly a shopping mall, but an entertainment centre at heart, this complex includes restaurants, a wine bar and a 10-screen cinema showing the latest films. If you feel like doing some shopping as well, it also offers a small selection of interesting options.

Beltissimo quality-driven but stylishly fashioned leather goods, shoes and handbags

Cerruti Jeans fashion based on natural and innovative fabric
Mexx a comfortable, stylish and trendy international line of clothing
Nautica apparel for the adventurous who want to be just as well dressed at the seaside as in the office

Wenceslas Square (Václavské Náměstí), Nové Město

Wenceslas Square is the retail hub of Prague, where you will find a large collection of department stores, neon signs and chain shops. Over the last century the square, once a beautiful Art Nouveau space, has largely been taken over by the emergence of modern stores. Between the mobile stalls and souvenir shops stand multiple 'high-street' outlets, including H&M, Debenhams and a giant Marks & Spencer.

Bata a large Czech-based store offering footwear for the entire family, as well as luggage and shoe repairs
Dum Mody five complete floors of Czech fashion to explore
M.A.C. known around the world for their quality, this shop offers the latest cosmetic collections
New Yorker a dominating, multi-level shop at the end of the square, offering cheap fashion for men, women and children
Nike the flagship store for the Czech Republic, with all of the standards and favourites
Palac Kinh the 'Palace of Books': a large bookshop arranged over several floors, with a sizable English language section and a good selection of international magazines
Promod women's fashion in a handsome, modern building on the corner, with some fun, different and sexy clothes
Sephora one stop for fashionable fragrance, cosmetic and skincare picks

STARE MĚSTO – THE OLD TOWN

Cerná Ruze, Na Příkopě, Staré Město
www.cernaruze.cz

The 'black rose' of Prague, the Cerná Ruze, is a shopping gallery that has been operating since the turn of the century. Located on this fashionable street, the centre houses a mix of Czech and international retailers. Set in a beautiful old palace (of which only the original façade remains), it is one of the more attractive centres, even if it's a bit too heavy on the bright lighting.

Elazar Leather high-quality funky leather bags, boots and jackets, for men and women
G-Star Raw denim of all styles for men and women
McGregor classic apparel for men – good for the casually smart city vibe
Moser Czech glass at its most ornate; this name is known for its stylish engraving techniques
Nova Fashion beautiful gowns and designs for women by Petra Kocianova
Pierre Cardin, Valentino, Guy Laroche a mixture of high fashion accessories and apparel available for men (there's also a Pierre Cardin shop for women's accessories and shoes on the first level of the centre)
Roberto Cavalli trendy and chic shoes and boots from this leading designer

Melantrichova, Staré Město

Located in the centre of tourists' Prague, Melantrichova is the main cut-through from Old Town Square to Wenceslas Square. The area includes some higher-end shops (a few carrying every form of crystal), but is overrun with tourist tack and people gawking at the entrance to the sex-machine museum.

Art Decoratif Art Nouveau trinkets and antiques housed in a shop copied from Mucha's work in Paris
Biailo expensive but excellent quality designer outerwear
Country Life possibly Prague's finest health food shop and café, carrying a range of international products – and over 25% of the stock is now certified organic
Manufaktura a must-stop when buying souvenirs for those unlucky

enough to not make the trip with you, this Prague staple (one of a chain in the city) offers old-fashioned wooden toys, a line of soaps and high-quality, unique souvenirs

Na Příkopě, Staré Město

One of the best shopping streets in the city, and recently ranked within the top 20 high streets in the world, Na Prikope is located at the bottom end of Wenceslas Square. The street is home to chic individual shops, including some high-end jewellery boutiques, the usual glass and tourist outlets, entrances to shopping complexes and ATMs for when you run out of cash.

Jackpot & Cottonfield smart Danish street wear for men and women
Lacoste classic French sportswear in a well-stocked, airy boutique
Leiser an extensive selection of shoes and boots for men and women, for days and nights in the city
Mango a well-distributed Spanish clothing company, producing reasonably priced fashion and accessories for women
L'Occitane en Provence French boutique carrying high-quality skincare products that look as fabulous as they smell
Salamander one outlet of a chain carrying a stylish selection of footwear
United Colours of Benetton the flagship Prague store, selling its ubiquitous collection of European fashions
Zara multiple levels of affordable funky Spanish fashion for men and women

U Prašné Brány, Staré Město

A small, stylish street behind the Municipal House, home to a selection of fashionable boutiques that are typical of the chic district of Josefov.

Kenzo French fashion and perfume in a discreet and intimate boutique
Leiser Teutonic practicality: German shoes for men and women
Mont Blanc pens, wallets and fashion accessories from this high-end, well-known line
Versace a shopping heaven for the style-conscious and wealthy, in a sump-

tuous setting

Wilvorst this line of shops offers 'retrofuturism clothing' – chic and sporty apparel for men and women

Železná, Staré Město

A small street leading from Old Town Square towards Wenceslas Square that's home to some small, designer boutiques. Zelezná isn't really worth a visit in itself, but is a convenient lane to wander down and window shop.

Allure offering inspired crystal selections and simple yet sophisticated jewellery pieces

Coccinelle high-fashion German handbags and shoes

Estéee Lauder high-quality cosmetic products from this renowned French house

Marina Rinaldi Italian designer producing sleek fashion for women

Stefanel relaxed and urban Italian men's and women's wear, from a relatively young global company

United Colors of Benetton this outlet carries only the children's and maternity collections of this popular brand

JOSEFOV

Pařížská, Josefov

Running off Old Town Square, Pařížská is the Champs-Elysées of Prague. This smart avenue is lined with designer shops and chic cafés, as well as more expensive tourist boutiques carrying antiques, crystal and jewellery. It can be explored by foot or in a horse-drawn carriage, and with the Jewish Quarter bisecting the street, is easily added to an afternoon of sightseeing. In addition to its flagship stores for the deluxe renowned fashions and styles of Boss, Dior, Hermès and Swarovski.

Alberto Guardiani a shoe-maker displaying modernity and refinement, creating shoes for the chic and adventurous

Alfred Dunhill a quintessentially British store selling stylish fashion that has transcended time

Bang & Olufsen a wide range of beautiful and high-quality electronics

Cartier unbounded elegance through French jewellery and watches

Ermenegildo Zegna some of the finest fashions in leather from this international brand

Francesco Biasia simply home to some of the finest and most elegant handbags in the city

Lacoste classic French sportswear in a well-stocked boutique

Le Patio an incredibly packed lifestyle shop carrying antique and oriental furniture, as well as new classics and stylish objects of every colour for the home

Lia Halada a sophisticated high-end jewellery collection from a Prague-based designer

Louis Vuitton luggage, leatherwear, handbags and fashion from a brand that is identifiable on every airport carousel

Michal Negrin an enchanting store offering romantic jewellery from an Israeli designer

Salvatore Ferragamo a selection of sophisticated shoes, clothing and leather goods from this elegant Italian designer

Shopping List

play...

There are alternatives to sightseeing! Why not spend some time soaking up the vibrancy of the city by watching a football match or an ice-hockey game, or getting a fresh perspective on city life from a hot-air balloon? After all, you're on holiday – seize the chance to do something unusual that you might not indulge in at home. Outdoor field sports enthusiasts can hunt for wild boar, duck or pheasants; adrenaline addicts can try kayaking, canoeing or maybe even sky-diving – in Prague you'll be able to find all sorts of companies, large and small, that can make it happen. For the less actively inclined, why not hire a small plane to check out the country's castles from the air?

The Czech Republic's two main sports are ice hockey and football, and going to a match can be an exhilarating (and seriously rowdy) experience. In the country that sent a gold-medal winning hockey team, as well as superstars Jaromir Jagr and Dominik Hasek, into the international hockey arena, you can find many rising talents playing on the ice of Prague. And if you want to delve further into the spirit of the new Republic, watch a football match on a Saturday surrounded by local fans.

In the summertime, spend some time walking along the river bank and the

parks that surround the city, you can hire a bicycle and ride to venture further afield than you might otherwise (but watch out for the tramways if you're on the streets).

You can also play a round of golf in the verdant countryside, or test your skills at an indoor driving range. In winter, you can go ice-skating on frozen reservoirs, which can prove particularly entertaining with the help of some grog from the local stalls.

Whether you've been parachuting over the city or spending a few hours at the races, take some time to relax in a spa, perhaps in Prague itself or in the sur-

rounding countryside if you've had enough excitement for a while. After all, between exploring the streets and culture of the city, eating at incredible restaurants, and yelling yourself hoarse at a hockey game, you deserve a break.

CYCLING

City Bike, Králodvorská 5, Stare Město
Tel: 077 618 0284 www.citybike-prague.com
Open: daily, 9am–7pm

City Bike is one of the few places in the centre of the city where you can
hire a bicycle for the day. Although cycling in Prague traffic can feel like a
serious adventure (always wear a helmet and watch out for the tram
tracks), there are some lovely parks where you can take a more leisurely
ride. City Bike will give you some good tips on where to go, as well as supply you with maps, helmets and even a free beer (best enjoyed after you
return the bike). If you're not comfortable navigating the city on your own,
they also offer a two-hour guided tour of the city that departs three times
daily.

FLYING

F-Air, Benesov Airport, Bystrice
Tel: 317 793 820 www.f-air.cz

Learn to fly, or simply hire a pilot and plane, and take a flight around the
beautiful Bohemian countryside, flying low over elegant castles and traditional villages (from 1,640kc for a 15-minute flight). Note that F-Air is located about 20 minutes outside Prague, so to get there, you'll have to take a
taxi or hire a car.

Ballooning, Na Vrcholu 7, Žižkov
Tel: 607 517 535 www.ballooning.cz

Ride in a hot-air balloon over the countryside and the small market towns
that typify the region. It's peaceful and slow, and a fantastic romantic option
– why not organize a champagne breakfast surprise for your loved-one? The
take-off is generally from Konopiste, and it's worth taking extra time to view
the castle. Prices range from 3,950kc upwards for a flight.

Tocna Airport
Tel: 241 773 454 (planes); 602 305 130 (balloons)

The airport can charter personalized sightseeing flights from this small airstrip at the edge of the city. Each plane can carry up to three passengers, but you need to book by phone at least two days in advance to set up a flight. Tocna can also offer hour-long flights over Prague in a balloon (weather permitting).

FOOTBALL

Football isn't the national game that it is in most European countries, even though the Czech team has been riding high in recent years. Domestic Czech teams rarely make it past the group stages of the Champions' League or the first couple of rounds of the UEFA cup, since most of their better players choose to play abroad in England, Germany and Italy. This means that the standard of play might be lower than expected, but matches can still be very entertaining and the Czech supporters are a passionate bunch.

AC Sparta Praha, Milady Horákové 98, Letná
Tel: 296 111 111 www.sparta.cz

The top team in the Czech Republic, although they have gone slightly downhill in recent years by European standards. You will probably see a good game in an impressive stadium, but the Premiership it's not. The evident skinhead element is worth avoiding – go for the more expensive seats. Tickets from 100kc.

CU Bohemians Praha, Vršovická 31, Vršovice
Tel: 274 771 806 www.fc-bohemians.cz

One of the smaller Prague teams, the Bohemians are popular more with ex-pats, and always seem to be on the brink of insolvency. The team play passionately, and are nicknamed 'The Kangaroos' – you'll have to ask them why.

FK Viktoria Žižkov, Seifertova 130, Žižkov
Tel: 222 722 045 www.fkvz.cz

This local Czech team has a tiny but loyal following. Since their stadium is reasonably close to the centre and has a friendly atmosphere, it is worth taking the time to pop along and double the crowd if you've got a few hours to catch a game. Tickets from 30kc.

SK Slavia Praha, Zatopkova 2, Strahov
Tel: 233 081 753   www.slavia.cz

SK Slavia Praha are undoubtedly skilled, although they are generally considered second to Sparta. This club is a favourite of the old republic and the middle classes.

GOLF

Golf is a relatively new sport in the country, hence good courses are few and far between. There is one 18-hole course near the centre of the city (Praha Karlstejn), and a 9-hole course in Praha 5, but there are other good courses surrounded by beautiful countryside (contact the Tourist Information Centre for further details, and bear in mind that you'll need a car to reach the golf courses). If you're feeling more like 'virtual golf', try out the new Erpet Golf Centrum.

Erpet Golf Centrum, Strakonická 4, P5
Tel: 257 321 177   www.erpet.cz

Aside from the tennis and squash courts, the Golf Centrum is home to golf simulators where you can 'play' 18 holes of golf (you can reserve these online). Simulators start from 300kc/hour, and opening hours vary depending on the season, so call beforehand. The Centrum also offers lessons, and has a two-storey driving range and a putting green.

Golf Club Praha, Plzenska 401/2, P5
Tel: 257 216 584   www.gcp.cz

Although the 9-hole course could be in better condition at some points, the club also has a driving range and is relatively easily accessible (about 7km from the centre of the city).

Praha Karlštejn Golf Klub, Běleč 272, Líteň
Tel: 311 604 991   www.karlstejn-golf.cz

A stunning 18-hole golf club, Karlstejn is located just outside the city. Set in beautiful countryside beneath an imposing castle, the course (designed by Canadian duo Les Furber and Jim Eremko) is a joy to play. Green fees range from 1,000 to 1,800kc, so it might not be as cheap as you'd hoped, but you can reserve a tee-off time online.

HORSE-RACING

Dostihový Spolek, Prazská 607, Pardubice
Tel: 466 797 111 www.pardubice-racecourse.cz

Although this course is located almost 70 miles east of Prague, there is a
bus service that will take you there. The track holds races every Saturday
from May to October, including the Velka Pardubicka steeplechase in
October (which has been run here since 1974). Tickets start at 110kc.

Velká Chuchle, Radotínská 69, P5
Tel: 257 941 431 www.velka-chuchle.cz

This is the main racecourse in the country and home to the Czech Derby
as well as international races such as the Grand Prix of Czech Turf, Grand
Prix of Prague and the President of the Republic's Prize. The course is located in the south-western suburbs of the city and easily reached by taxi.
Races are run every Sunday afternoon at 2pm throughout the season (April
to October), with a break in July. The bigger races are run in June and
October.

ICE HOCKEY

Ice hockey is the national sport of the Czech Republic, and fans are in fierce
competition with those of neighbouring Slovakia. Most games are well
attended, and can be quite ferocious at times. As with football, there are
two main teams in Prague, Sparta and Slavia, who have an intense rivalry.
Only the Sparta website offers information on games in English, but you can
check local newspapers for the dates of matches.

HC Slavia Praha, Vladivostocká 10, Vršovice
Tel: 267 311 417 www.hc-slavia.cz

This tiny stadium can get rowdy, with locals enjoying good games while
warming up the unheated arena with some serious spirit.

HC Sparta Praha, T–Mobile Arena, Za Elektrárnou 419, P7
Tel: 266 727 443 www.hcsparta.cz

The wealthier of the two hockey clubs, Sparta enjoys the luxury of its T-

Mobile arena, but the interior is now reflecting the use it has received since it was built. The spectators tend to get swallowed up into the space, but the hockey is worth coming out to watch – particularly when the playoffs are on.

ICE-SKATING

Ice-skating is very popular in the Czech Republic (which figures, since ice hockey is the national sport). Some of the hockey rinks are open to the public for few hours during the day in between hockey practices. In the winter, outdoor rinks are set up in the centre (check the local papers for details). Skaters may also to be found on the reservoirs at Divoká Sárka and Hostivar in the winter months, with stalls selling alcohol around the edge. If you want to skate in these areas, check the ice conditions first and hire skates in town before heading out.

HC Slavia Praha, Vladivostocká 10, Vršovice
Tel: 267 311 417 www.hc-slavia.cz

Private trainers are available, but only for groups. Call the rink for more information on ice times, or trainer Oldrich Helmich directly, on 602 325 484.

HC Sparta Praha, T-Mobile Arena, Za Elektrárnou 419, P7
Tel: 266 727 443 www.hcsparta.cz

Skating has been cancelled in past years due to flooding, so it's definitely worth calling ahead to see if you will be able to get ice time.

Stvanice, Ostrov Stvanice 1125, P7
Tel: 602 623 449 www.stvanice.cz

This structure, housing two rinks on Vltava island, is a bit worse for wear, but is open long hours. Check the website for details (follow the section called 'Verejne brusleni'). You can hire skates at the rink but might have to settle for a size up or down, since selection is limited.

University Sport Club, Zimni Stadion Hasa Samova 1, P10
Tel: 271 747 128

Connected to the Hotel Hasa, this rink is generally open from 9 to 11am. It's best to call before heading out, however, since there is talk of closure in the future.

KAYAKING and CANOEING

The Czech Republic's numerous rivers and steep hills make it ideal for kayaking. Here you can take the sport to whatever level you wish – gently paddle down a flat stream or drop off the edge of waterfalls and shoot the rapids. Just make sure that, as with all extreme sports, you have the expert ise to handle the rivers, and ask staff at the stores where you hire your gear for information on currents and water levels.

Boatpark, Sokolovská 146, Karlín
Tel: 284 826 787 www.boatpark.cz

You can hire or buy canoes here (generally at a slightly cheaper rate than above). Boatpark can deliver the boats at a rate of about 10kc per km and can advise on the best places to go.

Vodácký Ráj, Císařska Louka 27, Smíchov
Tel: 257 215 439   www.vodackyraj.cz

This sports equipment store on the west bank of the Vltava sells everything you need for kayaking at any level. They rent out canoes and can supply cars to take them to your chosen destination. Prices start from 160kc a day for a kayak only.

PARACHUTING

Aviatic Centrum Praha, Pujmanové 27, P4
Tel: 602 323 608 www.aviatic.cz

Jumping gives you a chance to really cut loose. At Aviatic you can learn to paraglide or parachute jump for rates that start at 4,450kc.

Paraskola Impact, Dolní 12, Nusle
Tel: 261 225 431 www.paraskolaimpact.cz

Impact offers courses for both beginners and advanced jumpers. The school has a good reputation, and also offers tandem jumps. Basic courses begin at 2000kc, which includes one jump.

Tandem Centrum, Na Pěkné Vyhlídce 4, Střešovice
Tel: 233 343 443 www.padaky.cz

For 3,500kc you can do a tandem parachute jump with a qualified instructor; for an extra 1,000kc they will video the event. If you wish to fulfil a burning desire to leap out of a plane at 4,000ft without any clothes on, then this is the place for you – they'll even film that, too.

SHOOTING and HUNTING

If you're looking for something a little different, try a day stalking deer and wild boar, or have them driven at you. There is always some element of risk involved, so it's not really recommended for those who have never handled a rifle or shotgun. Always remember to take ID with you to the range – your passport is best.

AVIM Praha, Sokolovská 23, Karlín
Tel: 222 329 328 www.avim.cz

This shooting range is located relatively close to the centre of town, and offers an advisor if you don't have a gun licence. If you're in the city with friends, they offer group programmes. Note that only some staff speak English. Open 10am–10pm daily.

Interlov Praha, Jungmannova 25, Nové Město
Tel: 272 659 355 www.interlov.cz

Interlov Praha organizes a range of hunting activities, offering you the opportunity to stalk roe, red, fallow and sika deer, chamois or wild boar. There are group hunts with driven wild boar shoots, and there is also small game, including pheasant, wild duck and hare. Interlov provides all that you will need, including insurance and licences – you have to email them at: info@interlov.cz for information on their services (including prices).

SSK Magnum Praha, Kamýcká 192, Sedlec
Tel: 233 322 466 www.magnumpraha.cz

You can learn how to shoot, stage competitions with your friends, and fire anything from a .44 Magnum to a semi-automatic Kalashnikov. Book ahead if you're coming here with a few people, since it's popular with stag groups.

SPAS

Worried about how many dumplings you've consumed, or just fancy a facial before a night at the opera? Prague's selection of spas has boomed in recent years, and new spots are to be found all over the city. If you're booking an entire day of pampering it's worth dropping by the spa beforehand to see the surroundings for yourself and meet the staff – that way you know you won't be disappointed. If you're really up for a treat, splurge on both time and money and enjoy the journey up to the celebrated spa town of Karlovy Vary.

Alchymist Hotel Spa, Tržiště 19, Malá Strana
Tel: 257 286 011   www.alchymisthotelresidence.com
Open: daily, 9am–9pm

The basement of this sophisticated hotel (see Sleep) is an atmospheric Balinese spa. The natural wood surroundings and quiet music are a nice touch, as is the team of professional Indonesian masseuses who offer a range of treatments and therapies, including Balinese, Roman and stone massages. There is also an adjacent fitness centre with a solarium.

Carlo IV Hotel Spa, Senovážné Náměstí 13, Nové Město
Tel: 224 593 111   www.boscolohotels.com
Open: daily, 9am–10pm

Located inside a luxury hotel (see Sleep), this spa includes a purifying sauna, large pool and Turkish bath. To top off the quiet surroundings, they also offer a selection of massages.

Cybex, Hilton Hotel, Pobřežní 1, Karlín
Tel: 224 842 375   www.cybexprg.cz
Open: daily, 6am (7am Sat/Sun)–10pm

With treatments so rich you could eat them, Cybex does not disappoint: here you'll be rolled, smeared and polished with mixtures of yoghurt, mud and mint gel. For true deluxe pampering go for the Cybex Special. Prices here are steep, but it's worth it.

Hotel Hoffmeister, Pod Bruskou 7, Malá Strana
Tel: 251 017 111 www.hoffmeister.cz
Open: daily, 8am–8pm

The Hoffmeister offers a unique stone bath in a cave spa originally dug out of rocky hillside in the 15th century. There's a broad variety of body and facial treatments and therapies as well as massages by certified masseurs and an Elizabeth Arden Beauty Centre.

Karlovy Vary (80 miles west of Prague)
Tel: 353 224 097 www.karlovyvary.cz

A few hours away by car or bus (four hours by train), the historic town of Karlovy Vary is known worldwide for its natural hot springs, spas and romantic settings. With over 10 springs to choose from, as well as a selection of baths, thermals and massages offered at a diverse range of luxurious spas, you need to plan ahead – check the town website for details of services available. Note, however, that many of these spas are not for the shy, as visitors often choose to use selected baths fully nude.

Mandarin Hotel Spa, Nebovidská 1, Malá Strana
Tel: 233 088 880 www.mandarinoriental.com
Open: daily, 9am–10pm

This beautiful spa, found inside the equally gorgeous Mandarin Hotel (see Sleep), features several treatment rooms built on the ancient remnants of a Gothic church. The remains can be seen below the glass floor as you enter the spa area to enjoy your vitality pool and water massage, or full range of beauty treatments.

Le Palais, U Zvonarky 1, Vinohrady
Tel: 234 634 670 www.palaishotel.cz
Open: daily, 7am–10pm

Le Palais offers a number of Swedish-style and hot-stone massage therapies with qualified masseurs. There's also a state-of-the-art whirlpool bath as well as a hydrojet, solarium, sauna, steam bath and aroma shower.

Sabai, Slovanský Dům, Na Příkopě 22, Nové Město

Tel: 221 451 180   www.sabai.cz
Open: daily, 10am–10pm

A Thai spa in the centre of Prague that is excellent value for money and offers a range of therapeutic and relaxation massages (starting at around 600kc for an hour). Sabai is an elegant little space, hidden above Na Prikope's busy shopping centre. It provides traditional massages, as well as special massages to relieve back pain and to improve the health and appearance of the skin.

Thai World, Týnská 9, Staré Město

Tel: 224 817 248   www.thaiworld.cz
Open: daily, 11am–9pm

Whether you feel in need of a relaxing traditional Thai massage or an invigorating complete reflexology session, the trained masseuses of Thai World will be able to meet your needs. The location can be cramped, however, and it's quite hot inside.

Zen Asian Wellness, V Jámě 6, Nové Město

Tel: 728 664 478   www.planetzen.cz
Open: daily, 10am–10pm

With a couple of outlets in Prague (one here and one situated in the Maximilian Hotel) Zen offers a relaxing list of traditional massages and treatments in relaxing and beautiful surroundings. Professional practitioners from South East Asia ply their trade with remarkable skill.

info...

DANGERS

There is very little to be wary of in Prague. Violent crime in the centre and tourist areas is virtually unheard of, but there are, nevertheless, stealthier members of the criminal fraternity who will always try to rip you off. Pickpockets are one such danger. Be especially careful in crowded areas such as on Charles Bridge, and always watch your bags and pockets as people clamber on and off the underground, trams and buses. The prostitutes around Wenceslas Square can be pretty insistent, too: don't be distracted by wandering hands; they might be after altogether different goods.

MONEY

The crown (CZK) is the unit of currency used in the Czech Republic. At the time of writing, the exchange rates are roughly: £1=43kc; $1=22kc; €1=28kc. Gone are the days when you had to worry about ordering travellers' cheques or wads of cash before you leave home. There are ATMs littered all over the centre of Prague; the first you'll come across will be at the airport. If you need large sums of money, these can be withdrawn from local banks on production of a passport. Try to avoid using a bureau de change, since you will inevitably get fewer crowns for your pounds, and never change money on the street – you will certainly be hustled.

NEWSPAPERS

A good source of information for cinema, theatre and event listings is the ex-pat bible, *The Prague Post*, available every Wednesday at the cost of 50kc. It can be picked up from all good newsstands and cafés, such as the Globe.

PUBLIC TRANSPORT

Public transport can be a little confusing. Tickets cannot be bought on buses or trams or even at some stops, but instead can be purchased from underground stations and yellow machines on street corners, or from a café, newsagent or tobacconist. Tickets have to be punched when you enter the underground, tram or bus in order to validate them, otherwise you may incur a 400kc fine if caught by an inspector (always ask to see their badge). A single non-transfer ticket, valid for 30 minutes on any form of transport, is 25kc; 24 hours cost 80kc, while a weekend sets you back 220kc. Underground, bus and tram maps are available from newsstands, tourist information offices and underground stations. Visit www.dp-praha.cz for more details.

TAXIS

Taxis are notoriously unreliable in Prague – if you pick them up in the street they will milk you for all they can, and there's pretty much nothing you can do about it. The best option is to call one of the local, reputable, English-speaking companies, who will pick you up from anywhere and won't overcharge you. A taxi from the airport will charge a fixed rate (around 650kc), while a taxi to the airport should cost you between 500 and 600kc. Taxi drivers are legally obliged to use their meters, but it is often far simpler to negotiate a fare before you get in. Both AAA (tel: 14014) and Profi Taxi (tel: 14035) are reliable companies.

TELEPHONES

All the telephone numbers in this book are given without the international code but retain the city code prefix. To call Prague from the UK, the international prefix is +420. The best way to make calls while in the city is to use your mobile, so remember to have you international option activated. Phone cards, which you can buy from the local newsagent, tobacconist or at your hotel, are a better option than trying to find a coin-operated payphone.

TIPPING

In restaurants and cafés it is best to round up the bill or add a 5 or 10% tip (and about the same for a taxi ride). Do not be afraid not to tip if the service is shoddy or you feel that you have been swindled.

index

index

index

index

index